Dawn of an Era
of Well-Being

Dawn of an Era of Well-Being

New Paths to a Better World

Ervin Laszlo
Frederick Tsao

Foreword by Deepak Chopra

A LASZLO INSTITUTE/AITIA INSTITUTE NEW PARADIGM BOOK

SelectBooks, Inc.
New York

This edition published by SelectBooks, Inc.
For information address SelectBooks, Inc., New York, New York.

First Edition

ISBN 978-1-59079- 515-6

Library of Congress Cataloging-in-Publication Data

Names: Laszlo, Ervin, 1932- author. | Tsao, Frederick, author.
Title: Dawn of an era of well-being : new paths to a better world / Ervin
 Laszlo, Frederick Tsao ; foreword by Deepak Chopra.
Description: First edition. | New York : SelectBooks, [2021] | "A Laszlo
 Institute / AITIA Institute New Paradigm Book." | Includes
 bibliographical references and index. | Summary: "Authors believe we can
 reverse humanity's destructive environmental path, positing that a new
 worldview of a "quantum paradigm" is emerging in society, based on
 awareness that consciousness is a universal energy field from which we
 form our reality—and guide civilizations to find solutions combining
 Western medicine and Eastern wisdom traditions to create better lives
 for all"— Provided by publisher.
Identifiers: LCCN 2021012510 (print) | LCCN 2021012511 (ebook) | ISBN
 9781590795156 | ISBN 9781590795163 (ebook)
Subjects: LCSH: Consciousness. | Cosmology. | Civilization--Forecasting. |
 Quantum theory. | Well-being.
Classification: LCC B808.9 .L365 2021 (print) | LCC B808.9 (ebook) | DDC
 128/.2--dc23
LC record available at https://lccn.loc.gov/2021012510
LC ebook record available at https://lccn.loc.gov/2021012511

Book design by Janice Benight

Manufactured in the United States of America
10 9 8 7 6 5 4 3 2 1

Contents

PART TWO

WESTERN AND EASTERN APPROACHES TO AN ERA OF WELL-BEING 45

PART THREE

PATHS TO THE NEW ERA 85

Foreword

by Deepak Chopra

As modern science finds new answers to the big questions facing us, the number of questions grows even faster, with a net result that ignorance is outstripping knowledge. At first sight this seems paradoxical. If you learn the vocabulary of a foreign language, it would be totally mystifying to learn that the words you don't know suddenly doubled.

But there's a reason behind the paradox. Science is exposing more questions than answers because, as fully explained by Ervin Laszlo and Frederick Tsao, there has always been a fatal flaw in the physicalist approach. For a long time, thanks to brilliant thinkers like Newton, Darwin, and Einstein, the flaw was kept at bay. By concentrating on the physical world, constant progress disguised the inability of science to account for the other half of human existence, our world "in here," the world of our consciousness.

Why would the chickens come home to roost just now, in our lifetime? It wasn't bad luck or accident. Instead, physics became so sophisticated that it found itself exploring the boundary where space, time, matter, and energy are created. At the same time, neuroscience is on the border of mapping the human brain's quadrillion connections. But the next step in both fields has stymied everyone. No matter how finely you examine either the cosmos or the brain, you cannot find a point where matter learned to think. As someone quipped, believing that matter can turn into mind is like asking a deck of playing cards to learn how to play poker.

It is a cause for embarrassed chagrin that science came so very close, within an iota of grabbing the biggest prize of all, the so-called Theory of Everything, suddenly to find that it was farther away than ever. It's exactly like a magician reaching for the rabbit he hid in his hat only to find that the rabbit took off without him seeing it. The purpose of this book is to rescue the future of science by doing what needed to be done all along—recognizing that both halves of reality, the world "out there" and the world "in here," belong to one whole and that this whole rests on the foundation of consciousness.

Since the job is well and thoroughly done by Laszlo and Tsao, I'd like to comment on only a single aspect of how a future worldview might look. I am going to focus on a single word, which is "space." The fact that this word holds the key to multiple mysteries looks far from obvious. One-word answers actually have a long tradition. If you wanted to answer any question, over the centuries you'd be told to rely on one word. In an age of faith the word was God; today it is science. Other one-word possibilities have had their appeal: reason is big, so is love. "All you need is love" is a Beatles lyric that moves the heart, and at the other end of the spectrum, cosmologists searching for a Theory of Everything to unite the fundamental forces in nature stake their hopes on their favorite word, mathematics.

But in many ways space is the one word that satisfies the clashing claims of love, reason, God, and science. Space allows us to embrace all of them. Here's how the argument goes. In between every thought there is a gap, a space that divides mental activity into discrete feelings, sensations, images, and thoughts. Spacing makes separate words intelligible. We inhabit a personal space that we don't like others to intrude upon. Outer space contains every physical object in creation. Inner space is the domain of the psyche. Between them, the space "out there" and "in here" embraces all of existence.

Indeed, even each letter defines the spaces between it and the letters to either side. Jewish mystics speak of the "other alphabet" of the spaces between the Hebrew letters of the scriptures. What gives space its real potency is mysterious. The gap between thoughts isn't empty. It is the womb of the mind. No one knows where a thought comes from, but the place must be empty of thought. An artist's mind isn't a collection of paintings but the source of possible paintings. So space is the place where possibilities exist. (Calling the mind a space is very old, going back to the Sanskrit term *Chit Akash*, where *Akash* means space and *Chit* is conscious awareness.)

How can empty space contain the possibility of anything, much less everything? That's a question the thinking mind cannot answer, because thinking is a process that shoots you out of pure space (pure awareness) into the mind's bustling activity. This sounds like metaphysics, but there is a tantalizing clue in the space inside your body, which is much closer to home. Once microscopes were invented, it could be seen that the body is made up of cells. Looking carefully, one observes that every cell derives from a prior cell. But are our bodies only cells, one vast, solidly packed cluster and nothing else? No. Because while many cells are tightly clustered together, many are not.

There are spaces between some cells (in the skin, for example, where the spaces allow your body to absorb moisture), though not between others (the digest tract lining is tightly bound, in order to keep in-flow and out-flow tightly controlled). There are bigger spaces around capillaries, the tiniest blood vessels, where nutrients are delivered to cells and the cells' waste taken away. These spaces are called *interstitial spaces*, literally the "between." Holding all this emptiness together is fibrous tissue made up of different types of collagens and other large molecules, which are stiff or elastic, allowing things in the body to both stay where they are and move when they need to.

We think of space as the emptiness that separates things. Interstitial spaces look empty on a microscope slide, but they are filled with fluid and molecules. They probably conduct electricity, and some cells live and travel through them. On the cosmic scale outer space isn't empty either, but is more alive than anything in the visible universe. Nothing in creation is disconnected from everything else. When a group of physicists and cosmologists was asked to name the one concept they could all agree upon, the answer they came up with was *unboundedness*. To a quantum physicist, the physical universe has a deeper level where nothing exists but invisible waves or ripples in the quantum field.

These ripples have no edges or boundaries. They are said to collapse in order to appear in the physical domain as objects we can see, touch, and investigate. But the real womb of the universe is known as a mathematical space (Hilbert space). Mathematics would seem to define the ultimate space, but there's another step to go. Mathematics is still a construct in the mind, and we can't claim to find the ultimate space until we go beyond mind-made constructs. All trails eventually lead to some kind of meta-space. The agreed-upon word for it is consciousness (although many scientists are still putting their eggs into the basket of materialism, preferring to leave consciousness out of the discussion). Consciousness is so different from outer space that it isn't obvious why "space" is a useful term for it. In fact, the word "space" is only useful to give a general sense of things, the lay of the land. No words actually describe consciousness.

Consciousness precedes thought. "I think, therefore I am" doesn't go far enough. "I am aware, therefore I am" is better. You don't have to be thinking to be aware. Babies are very aware without any words in their heads. It seems fair to say that consciousness is aware of itself, and nothing else, no complex philosophical explanation or religious doctrine, is needed. A few other things go along with "I am aware, therefore I am." You are here in the now. You are alive. With life comes thinking, feeling, and doing. These things are so basic that we rarely talk about them. But the questions I've touched on (modestly lumped together in Douglas Adams's comical *Hitchhiker's Guide to the Galaxy* as Life, the Universe, and Everything) occur in the space known as consciousness. Pure consciousness doesn't do anything. Invisibly, secretly, it holds possibilities, an infinite number of them, that will manifest as reality.

Thanks to this space known as consciousness, no matter how many ideas, feelings, artworks, dreams, discoveries, and imaginary fancies human beings come up with, an infinite number will remain. Possibilities, like the universe, are unbounded. The whole reason for finding a one-word answer has always been the same: to explain ourselves to ourselves. This book shows how the future might gain in self-awareness, which is totally necessary. In this book the authors, Ervin Laszlo and Frederick Tsao, solve many mysteries and shed light on the path we can take toward a better world. But even more than this, they point to the path for shifting to a new paradigm of consciousness so that our ailing planet can be healed—because without this leap in consciousness, it won't happen.

An Introductory Note from the Authors

This book explores new paths toward creating a better world: an era of well-being. The authors and contributors explore both the contemporary science-based typically Western approach to this objective and the tradition-based, and now actively revived, Chinese and generally Eastern approach. The invited thought leaders explore a further variety of creative paths. All these paths and approaches converge conclusively towards a holistic view of the world as the necessary foundation of human well-being.

Humankind today is facing monumental challenges—the sustainability of natural resources, climate change, wealth inequalities, breakdowns in social structures, the impact of artificial intelligence, and of course the threat of pandemics. The COVID-19 pandemic is an example of how the universe is constantly rebalancing itself to offset forces moving in contradiction to its natural energy, which in Chinese culture is called the *Dao*. An impact of the virus has been to slow us down and force us all to reflect, to open our eyes to the need for change, to see that a new normal is both required and also imminent. And the crisis also showed that we can heal if we choose a new way. We were sitting at home—working, studying, and reflecting—and not only were we watching the chaos of the world outside, we were also awakening to the divisiveness that created the chaos. The virus has also given rise to a whole new unifying energy amidst the divisiveness, with people tackling the global challenge of the virus problem regardless of economic or political pressure. We realized that Earth can heal itself if left alone and that mindful living and well-being are what are needed to regain a balance. The time has arrived for a global integration and upgrade of human civilization based on a new and more reliably grounded view of the world.

The main challenge that has been highlighted is that of our sustainability. In a way it is a gift and a blessing that the pandemic has thrown the issues before us in sharp contrast. We know now, more than ever before, that we must change or perish. Worldviews are the foundation of culture, and the crisis has presented us with an opportunity to move to a new worldview linking ancient and modern, East and West, science and spirituality. Endowed with technology and a new worldview informed by ancient wisdom as well as the findings of contemporary science, we can create a new narrative and witness the dawn of a better era.

It is clear that we are at a crossroads. We have a choice—either to continue down the road beset by many crises caused by divisiveness and separation or find the road toward unity, well-being, and thriving. Change is needed on all levels: change for the individual, change for society, and change in the consciousness that defines what we do and who we are. It is imperative that we achieve constructive change on all levels if we are to avoid even greater crises heading our way with the direst of consequences.

It is easy to be overwhelmed by a sense of chaos, but amidst the chaos lies the possibility for connecting with each other, reconnecting to our roots, and creating a shift in our consciousness. Now we can set about creating a new and better era for the human family, an era marked by individual and collective well-being.

This task and possibility inspires and motivates the ideas put forward in this book. It is the hope and expectation of the authors that they will prove to be of practical value as the human community sets about the monumental task of building a better world, rising from the global health crisis as a phoenix rises from the ashes of the past.

Preface

A New Paradigm for Thought and Action

The new paradigm discussed in this book impacts on human life in all its aspects, and its impact on healing and health are of particular significance. New branches in the sciences now research, develop, and hone the tools we need to create a higher level of well-being for all. Agreement regarding the basic aspects of our view of the world is essential, since the conflicts we experience arise from divergences in our values and beliefs and sense of identity. We need a common narrative to guide us in our shared evolution. We can evolve such a narrative when we agree on our basic aspirations for life. Common sense, which has become the rarest of senses in today's world, will return when we focus on how we live, because in the end the quality of our life is the basis for all we have and all we will have.

We now hold the power to shape our destiny. Our task is not to predict the future but to create it. Because of the chaos and crisis created by the pandemic we can now create a shift in consciousness as an essential condition of the shift to a new world.

Our priority must be to orient this shift so that it produces developments that do not let us fall back into the old pattern but move us forward toward a new world. We need to awaken to the opportunity granted us and make sure that we do not go against the evolutionary trend. If we attempted to do so, we would suffer the consequences.

But we have good reason to believe that we shall not fail to seize the opportunity opening for us. There is an awakening in progress in the world, a realization that things are very different from what they have been. Through the pandemic and the conditions it has provoked, the world has changed profoundly. It is as if we were caught in a body that does not belong to us anymore and are trying to break free; yet we are afraid. It is as if we were sitting in water that is getting hotter and hotter and moving toward the point where we have no option but to leap out or get burned.

There are signs that we are waking up. The United Nations, a body established to bring the nations of the world together, is rising to a new resonance in their objectives that govern the affairs of its member states. From the establishment of the Millennium Development Goals, the UN progressed to having Sustainable Development Goals and then called for a new economic paradigm to replace traditional objectives of capitalism with an economic philosophy centered on well-being and happiness. We are now in a time of recognizing the reality of a global shift in our worldview and trying to cope with it. Business and consumer trends reflect this shift along with the growth of a wellness industry.

Perhaps the most significant developments are the speed of revolution in technology and the emergence of a new science of consciousness and life. These pave the way to enable us to create a new era of well-being. We need a system for the governance of life on the planet that supports the growing realization that the old system is obsolete, and we must find a better one. There are signs that a better system is already emerging. The world is changing at an accelerated rate. News and information are available today in the blink of an eye, almost instantaneously worldwide. The challenge of our time is to use the opportunity for change to explore the conditions for well-being for all members of the human family.

We are changing, but how? Where are we headed? Many say that it is toward a new normalcy. But normalcy in the established sense is what we have put in place to protect ourselves from change. The pandemic has been an opportunity, amidst the enforced stillness, to reflect on overcoming the old normalcy and finding a new normalcy—the normalcy of well-being and flourishing in life. This is an opportunity to consider what is truly important in our life, to examine our actions and what the purpose of our life is. The sudden period of intense stillness allows us to make choices about how we want to live and confirm our life's highest priorities.

As we look around us, feeling the pulse of change as it appears in the social media and in the daily news, we realize that underneath the surface conflicts, crises, and periodic catastrophes, positive trends also are unfolding. These trends need to be recognized and reinforced. We must acknowledge the interconnections that underlie our life and constitute the foundation of the world. We are part of this world, and we cannot be well in this world until the world itself is well—meaning that it is basically and essentially integral and whole. Wholeness is an essential factor in the world. This has been recognized by the world's spiritual systems, the wisdom expressed in traditional cultural practices and is now validated by insights coming to light at the forefront of the sciences.

In this book, we explore the paradigm that will allow us to recognize the wholeness that is underneath the conflict and the divisiveness of the everyday world. This paradigm is the fruit of the integration of the many remarkable insights that come to light at the leading edge of the contemporary natural sciences. Bowing to the pioneering role of the quantum sciences in articulating this paradigm, we call it "the quantum paradigm." This is the fundamental scheme of thought that provides reliable guidance as we set about exploring the approaches that could bring us toward a new and better world.

We first sketch the contours of the world mapped by this paradigm, and then explore both the Western scientific and the Eastern spiritual approach to creating an era of well-being on this planet.

PART ONE

Shifting to a New World

The Relevance of the Quantum Paradigm

CHAPTER 1

Context for the Rise of the New Paradigm

Our current era, the industrial era, is hallmarked by a worldview based on science. However, science is changing, and the worldview based on it must change as well. This change is now imperative: the classical but still dominant view is obsolete. It conceives of the world in the dualistic mode of body and spirit, of science and spirituality, where science is counterposed to spirituality, and physical reality dominates—and in fact excludes—consciousness. Humanity needs to shift toward a view that overcomes these dualisms and offers an integral perspective on nature, life, and consciousness. This is the worldview warranted by the new paradigm, based on insights coming to light at the cutting edge of the quantum sciences.

In part one we outline the contours of the world mapped by the new "quantum" paradigm. But first we place this paradigm in the context of the overall evolution of contemporary thought.

The Evolution of Worldviews from the First to the Fourth Industrial Revolution

Consciousness is a decisive facet of the new paradigm. The worldview of the emerging paradigm takes us beyond the bounds of the first of the modern-age revolutions known as the First Industrial Revolution.

Although the first industrial revolution began as early as 1760, its impact on human life and society has been enormous, with wide implications for the coming era. It created major advances in technology, especially in regard to the inventing of machines that serve the demand for industrial and consumer products. This was an era characterized by Newtonian science; it was a mechanistic, deterministic, and materialistic paradigm which drove the classical processes of industrialization. It created vast advances in engineering and technology, and it developed the system of capitalism.

In the late 20th century, and presently in the third decade of the 21st century as we enter the fourth industrial revolution, it has become apparent that the Newtonian paradigm is no longer able to meet the needs of humanity. The explosion of population, social discrimination, economic gaps, geo-political instability, religious conflicts, natural disasters, and health crises all point towards the crisis of a world operating on the basis of the Newtonian mechanistic paradigm.

The First Industrial Revolution was based on the harnessing of steam. It was followed by the Second Industrial Revolution based on the uses of electricity, and this was followed by the Third Industrial Revolution based on information and driven by the development of the information sciences. The revolution of information is now reaching a point where technological advancement enabled the invention of machines that can outperform human beings in speed and precision. This progress in technology marked the advent of the Fourth Industrial Revolution hallmarked by artificial intelligence. Our Fourth Revolution will continue to reshape technology and revolutionize human life on the planet, blurring the distinction between physical, digital, and biological systems and processes.

Now that we have moved into the Fourth Industrial Revolution, our life on Earth is in flux. Global warming, racism, political and climate refugees, the accumulation of CO_2 and toxins in the air, water, and soil, are many potential crisis-points waiting to be actualized. If we are not to suffer multiple crises with unforeseen and at this time unforeseeable consequences, we must reflect on who we are, and how we relate to the world around us. We need to ask deep existential questions and follow up the best answers we can reach regarding them. We must be aware that the choices we make today address the real issues and not their superficial symptoms. We must stop attempting stop-gap measures that merely to plug the most visible holes but do not change the structures, systems, and processes that created the problems.

We cannot fit a system that served the mechanistic worldview into a holistic nonmechanistic conception of the world. This would be like trying to fit a square peg into a round hole.

A new structure and system have to be constructed instead of trying to mend the old, broken system. We need to promote and articulate the *Fourth Industrial Revolution*, a transformation which forms a revolution not only in technology but in worldview—above all in the structure of human consciousness.

INDICATIONS OF THE BIRTH OF A NEW CULTURE[1]

There are movements at the creative margins of society that confirm that we are about to transcend the boundaries of the Fourth Industrial Revolution. These movements augur the birth of a fundamentally new culture. Culture in this context means the ensemble of the values, worldviews, and aspirations that characterize a group of people and distinguish it from others.

Today, the biology of the human family is the same as it has been throughout recorded history, but its culture is not the same. Every society has its own culture, and this culture is changing from generation to generation. In our time, it is changing even within the lifetime of the now living generation. The emerging culture is seldom clear, distinct, and uncontested. It is usually segmented among several layers. Today there is a youth culture, an academic culture, a traditional culture, a simple life-culture, and many more. There is a mainstream culture at the center and various subcultures at the periphery.

In the present period, a wide variety of subcultures are born—and die—at the periphery. Some of them hold great promise. The most promising subculture is pioneered by people who abandon outdated beliefs and loosen the grip of the past on society. The leading minds of these cultures shift from a mindset of consumption based on quantity toward one based on quality defined by environmental sustainability. They adopt a worldview of holistic well-being, rejecting the negative characteristics of the mainstream culture.

The movement from the old to the new culture is indicated by a number of basic shifts in in the way people think and act. California's Institute of Noetic Sciences (IONS) enumerated the following shifts:

- *The shift from competition to reconciliation and partnership:* a change from relationships, organizational models, and societal strategies based on competition to relationships and models based on the principles of healing, reconciliation, forgiveness, and male-female partnership.

- *The shift from greed and scarcity to sufficiency and caring:* a change in values, perspectives, and approaches from the traditional self-centered and greedy mode toward a sense of the sufficient and the interpersonal concern of caring.

- *The shift from outer to inner authority:* a change from reliance on outer sources of "authority" to inner sources of "knowing."

- *The shift from separation to wholeness:* a recognition of the wholeness and interconnectedness of all aspects of reality.

- *The shift from mechanistic to living systems:* a shift of attention from models of organizations based on mechanistic systems to perspectives and approaches rooted in the principles that inform the world of the living.

- *The shift from organizational fragmentation to coherent integration:* a shift from disintegrative, fragmented organizations with parts set against each other to goals and structures integrated so they serve both those who participate in the organizations and those around them.

A basic and highly promising shift concerns the assessment of value. The traditional and still mainstream culture associates value with money and power. To be successful is the aim of life, and success is to be wealthy and powerful. This applies to individuals as well as to entire societies conceived as economic systems. The culture of mainstream economics is based on the Gross National Product as the criterion. Fortunately, the hold of GNP-based culture is loosening. A number of alternatives are emerging—doing so timidly and with a limited hold over people's minds. Now the crisis wrought by the virus pandemic impels people to consider them, knowing there is a need for alternatives. The following are the most notable of the alternatives subcultures:

Value Defined by Gross National Happiness

The term "Gross National Happiness" was coined in 1972 by King Jigme Singye Wangchuck of Bhutan when he declared, "Gross National Happiness is more important than Gross Domestic Product." Development needs to take a holistic approach and give equal importance to economic and to more subtle non-economic aspects of well-being.

In 2012, Bhutan's Prime Minister Jigme Thinley and UN Secretary-General Ban Ki-Moon convened the *High Level Meeting: Well-being and Happiness: Defining a New Economic Paradigm* to encourage the spread of Bhutan's GNH philosophy. At the High Level meeting, The first World Happiness Report was issued. Shortly thereafter the International Day of Happiness was proclaimed by the United Nations.

Unlike GNP, GNH sets collective happiness as the goal of governance, emphasizing harmony with nature and respect for traditional values and practices. According to the Bhutanese government, the four pillars of GNH are:

sustainable and equitable socio-economic development

environmental conservation

preservation and promotion of culture

good governance

Governance by the Happy Planet Index

The Happy Planet Index (HPI) was introduced by the New Economics Foundation in 2006. It is an index of human well-being and environmental impact. Each country's HPI value is a function of its average subjective life satisfaction, life expectancy at birth, and ecological footprint per capita. The index is weighted to give progressively higher scores to nations with low ecological footprints. Sustainable development is said to require taking account of the environmental costs of pursuing socio-economic goals.

The HPI is designed to challenge established indices of national development. GDP is considered inappropriate as an indicator of value, given that the ultimate aim of people is not to be rich but to be healthy and happy.

Value defined by the Genuine Progress Indicator

The "genuine progress indicator" (GPI) is a metric to replace, or at least to supplement, GDP. The indicator is designed to take fuller account of well-being in a nation, only a part of which is accounted for by its economy. The GPI factors in environmental and carbon footprints, including forms of resource depletion, pollution and long-term environmental damage. GDP increases twice when pollution is created, since it increases upon the creation of pollution (as a side-effect of some otherwise valuable process) and again when the pollution that was created is cleaned up. In contrast, GPI counts the initial pollution as a loss (rather than a gain) generally equal to the amount it will cost to clean it up, plus the cost of other negative effects of the pollution. In accounting for the costs borne by society in repairing or controlling pollution as well as poverty, GPI balances GDP spending as external costs.

If these shifts and developments are a trustworthy indication of current sociocultural trends, major change is on the horizon in many societies, especially in those that can afford to experiment with alternative modes of organization and acting. Many of the new subcultures emerging at the periphery are intensely hopeful. When a critical mass will subscribe to them, a new era will dawn for the human family, an era hallmarked by a higher level of well-being.

FOUR FUNDAMENTAL QUESTIONS ABOUT LIFE AND WELL-BEING

If contemporary societies are to find the path toward an era of higher well-being, four fundamental questions need to be raised. We raise these questions here and assess them first in the context of the current understanding offered by Western science (chapter three), and then in light of the traditional wisdom of China and the East (chapter four). The four questions are:

What is the science of life?

What is the purpose of life?

What is the condition we call well-being? and

what is the true nature of healing and health ?

1. What is the "science" of life?

Life itself is both a science and an art. The art of life has found expression in both Eastern and Western cultures. Life science is the contemporary science dedicated to investigating the structures and processes of life. Life itself is a process that produces ever larger and more complex and coherent structures: whole systems.

Today's life science is a branch of science that includes biology, medicine, and in its outreach also anthropology and sociology. It is focused on the investigation of living organisms and the vital structures and processes of living organisms.

2. What is the purpose of life?

As shown by the processes of development we observe in nature, we can most reasonably maintain that the purpose of life is the flourishing of the forms and processes that express life—the growth and development of living beings.* Organisms are systems, and organisms collectively create wider "supersystems." They are multilevel systems—systems composed of other systems. They evolve in interaction with other systems in the biosphere of the planet.

7.8 billion humans collectively constitute a bio-social and bio-ecological system, just as the 37.4 trillion cells in our body constitute the system of our organism. We can think of the overall system constituted by human beings as a system of life, a dynamic evolving system that seeks to expand and flourish. In the current epoch, the system of life on this planet is expanding and seeks expansion ever further, even to other parts of the solar system.

A new branch of life science is emerging that is focused on consciousness. It covers a wide range of disciplines from epigenetics and evolutionary biology to neuroscience, integral philosophy, and experimental parapsychology.

---

* This proposition is explored in detail in Ervin Laszlo, *My Journey* (New York: Select-Books, 2021).

The emerging science perceives the nature of life itself, and the nature of life as manifested in the organism, as essentially evolutionary. Evolutionary life science is expanding the existing boundaries of science, challenging the conventional limits of the paradigm that has dominated scientific thought until recently.

3. What is the condition we call well-being?

The new evolutionary life science sees humanity itself as a system, but it realizes that it is not the whole system. Humanity is a subsystem in the biosphere, and the biosphere in turn is a subsystem in the embracing system of life on this planet.

The essential realization is that humanity is a system within wider systems. The evolution of the human system is not preordained. The seven billion people-cells of the human system could evolve either into a wider life-enhancing system, or into a planetary cancer. In order to guide the human system toward its life-enhancing development, every human being needs to play a conscious role, constantly adjusting his and her structures and processes to be in harmony with Earth's biosphere— the highest complex and coherent system to emerge in this region of the universe. This is the path to an era of well-being.

Humanity is a living system and an expression of the drive intrinsic to nature and evolution. We have the potential to become a highly advanced expression of this drive. If we become that, we will have the power to create our own future. We need to awaken and align with the evolutionary impulse: that is the key to our well-being. If we do not awaken from our slumbers and continue to feed the forces of self-centeredness and separation, the evolutionary impulse will find its own path of development, and the system of life on this planet will realign itself without the participation of humanity.

4. What is the true nature and health and healing?

The new paradigm emerging in science has clear and crucial application to the field of health and healing. In the modern mainstream, the basic objective of doctors and healers has been the maintenance of health more than the treatment of disease. Doctors and healers are called in when the subjects are sick. In the traditional cultures, on the other hand, healers are often called in while the subjects are still healthy in order to *keep* them healthy.

Contemporary Western and Western-style medicine is more accomplished in curing disease than in maintaining the organism in a condition of good health. It seeks to correct cellular and organic malfunctions by biochemical and, if necessary, surgical means. Western medicine's remarkable achievements have prolonged human life expectancy and eliminated or produced cures for a plethora of diseases.

If modern medicine is to respond to the needs of our day, it needs to extend its focus to the maintenance of health beyond the cure of disease. And today's medicine needs to go beyond a focus on the diseased or dysfunctional part to the whole organism in its physical, biochemical, and socio-psychological environment. This enlargement calls for taking into account the flows and balances that ensure health and vitality in the organism, rather than concentrating on the causes of malfunction in a part.

The limitations inherent in Western and Western-style medicine can be overcome by observing, measuring, and analyzing the energetic and informational interactions that maintain health in the whole organism. The new sciences of life testify to the presence of complex and coordinated flows of energy and information embracing the whole organism. Maintaining these flows in functional order is essential for the well-being and even for the survival of the organism. The healers of traditional societies knew this and concentrated on maintaining the flows of energy in functional order. They developed a wide range of curative substances and practices designed to overcome blockages and malfunctions. Until the rise of recent interest in natural substances and methods, many of these traditional substances and practices have been disregarded, if not dismissed as mere superstition.

Currently the newest branches of modern medicine have begun to investigate the curative potentials of natural flows of energy both within the organism and between the organism and its natural and social environment. The latest developments signal a return to a holistic approach to the cure of disease and the safeguarding of health. They redefine the very nature of health and well-being—as summarized under the following points.

- Health is a dynamic balance in the living organism; it is the condition in which it properly processes the information required for its persistence in its environment.

- Disease is a pathology of the system-governing information, a flaw in the processing of information by the organism.

- A disease is simultaneously an individual and a collective condition. It is individual when limited to an individual subject but, given that all organically caused medical conditions are multidimensionally connected, such limitation is never absolute. Recognizing that a disease is a collective condition is essential for correctly diagnosing and treating it.

The crisis we are experiencing today is not just a crisis of health, but a crisis of the paradigm dominating the practice of healing and medicine. Science in the new era will bring a new model of well-being. It will be defined by systems concepts mapping living systems and orienting them toward healthy life and living. Consumerism causing environmental degradation and other economic and social problems derives from a worldview that is no longer valid and needs to change. We need a worldview that promotes the shift from a system of wastage to a system that redistributes resources to be accessible to all humanity and not only to a select few.

In the new era founded on the principles of the emerging paradigm, everything is integrated in the framework of larger wholes, and the embracing whole-system includes the nonphysical aspects of existence as well as its physical aspects. In the West, the development of the nonphysical aspects is still in its early stages, while in the East these aspects have received serious attention for thousands of years.

We have sufficient knowledge and resources as well as effective access to the needed resources to meet the material needs of the human family. We need to embrace the new paradigm emerging in the sciences to enable us to meet also the nonphysical aspects of our existence. Then the dawn of an era of well-being will give rise to an era of billiant daylight.

CHAPTER 2

Insights from the Quantum Paradigm

NEW CONCEPTS OF THE NATURE OF REALITY

As recognized fields of science, the quantum disciplines are radically new. The insights they offer are very different from the Newtonian as well as the Darwinian conceptions of the world. These insights are becoming more widely known, but they have still a long way to travel. A materialist-mechanistic view still holds sway in the thinking of the general public. Most people believe that the universe is a soulless mechanism, and life is a random accident. From that viewpoint the specific features of living species result from a succession of accidental events in the history of biological evolution on this planet, and the features of human beings are due to a fortuitous combination of the genes with which they were born. The psyche, in turn, is dominated by elemental drives for survival and sexual and other forms of self-gratification.

This, however, is not the concept of the emerging quantum paradigm. The popular ideas of Newton, Darwin, and Freud, the basic sources of today's purportedly scientific views of nature and the human being have been overtaken by new discoveries. In the worldview of the emerging quantum paradigm the universe is not a lifeless, soulless aggregate of inert chunks of matter; it resembles a living organism more than a dead rock. Life is not a random accident, and the basic drives of the human psyche include far more than drives for survival and self-gratification.

There is a radically new concept of the world taking shape in the quantum sciences, and in the following section we present these new elements.

The Nature of Matter

The emerging quantum paradigm changes the most fundamental idea we have of reality—our idea of what matter is. In the classical Newtonian view, matter and space coexist: they are the ultimate furnishings of reality. Matter occupies space and moves about in it, and space is a backdrop or container. This classical concept was radically revised in Einstein's relativistic universe—where spacetime became an integrated four-dimensional manifold—and again in Nils Bohr's and Werner Heisenberg's quantum physics. In light of what quantum scientists are beginning to realize about the nature of the space that is the background of matter, they think it's no longer warranted to view matter as primary and space as secondary. It is to space—or rather, to the cosmically extended "zero-point field" of the quantum vacuum—that the quantum paradigm grants primary reality.

The reason for the shift from matter to energy as the primary reality lies in the discovery that, notwithstanding its name, the quantum vacuum is not an empty space—a "vacuum"—but a filled space: a plenum. It is the locus of the zero-point field, so named because the energies of this field become manifest when all other energies vanish: at the zero point.

In itself, this primordial field is not electromagnetic, gravitational, or nuclear. Instead, it is the originating source of the known electromagnetic, gravitational, and nuclear forces and fields. It is also the originating source of the matter particles themselves. By stimulating the zero-point field of the vacuum with sufficient energy—of the order of 10^{27} erg/cm^3—a particular region of it is "kicked" from the state of negative into the state of positive energy. This makes for "pair-creation": Out of the vacuum emerges a positive energy (real) particle with a negative energy (virtual) particle twin remaining in it.

The energy density of the zero-point field is almost inconceivable. According to John Wheeler, it works out in light of Einstein's mass-energy equation $E = mc^2$ to 10^{94} gram/cm^3. But a density of 10^{94} gram per cubic centimeter is greater than the total matter density of the universe. The latter is merely 10^{-29} gram/cm^3! It is fortunate, then, that the energies of the vacuum are "virtual." Otherwise—since energy is equivalent to mass and mass carries gravitation—this superdense universe would instantly collapse to a size smaller than the radius of an atom.

The observable universe is not a *solidification* of vacuum energies, but a *thinning* of it—a one-hundred and eighty degree shift from the idea that matter is dense, autonomous, and moving in passive and empty space.

Matter is an emergent in this nearly infinite virtual energy field. The matter that furnishes the observable universe was created when the vacuum became destabilized in the explosion known as the big bang. The enormous energies liberated by this brought forth pairs of particles from the vacuum, and those that did not annihilate each other made up the matter content of the universe. Scientists now know that not only in its origins, but also in its behavior, matter in the universe conserves close connections with the vacuum field.

The inertial force itself may be due to interactions with the zero-point field. In a study first published in 1994, Bernhard Haisch, Alfonso Rueda, and Harold Puthoff gave a mathematical demonstration that inertia can be considered a vacuum-based Lorentz force. The force originates at the sub-quantum level and produces opposition to the acceleration of material objects. The accelerated motion of objects through the vacuum produces a magnetic field, and the particles that constitute the objects are deflected by this field. The larger the object the more particles it contains, hence the stronger the deflection—and greater the inertia. Inertia is thus a form of electromagnetic resistance arising in accelerated frames from the distortion of the virtual-particle gas of the vacuum.

More than inertia, mass can also be considered a product of vacuum interaction. If Haisch and his collaborators are right, the concept of mass is neither fundamental nor even necessary in physics. The vacuum contains massless charges of bosons that make up the superfluid zero-point field. Mass is effectively "created" when these massless charges interact with the electromagnetic field beyond the threshold of 10^{27} erg/cm^3. Thus mass may be a structure condensed from vacuum energy, rather than a fundamental given in the universe.

If mass is a product of vacuum energy, then so is gravitation. Gravity, as we know, is always associated with mass, obeying the inverse square law (it drops off proportionately to the square of the distance between the gravitating masses). Hence if mass is produced in interaction with the vacuum, the force that is associated with mass is also produced. This suggests that *all* the fundamental characteristics we associate with matter are products of vacuum interaction: inertia, mass, and also gravity.

In the quantum paradigm matter is viewed as a product of interaction with the vacuum's zero-point field. As Max Planck himself said in one of his last lectures in Florence, in the last count, matter as such does not exist in the universe.

The Nature of Life

The quantum paradigm also fundamentally changes our concept of life. Life is not the introduction of a new and alien element in the physics of the universe. It is part of the evolutionary process that unfolds in the space and time of the universe. Some particles of "matter"—which in the final count are matter-like vibrations in the zero-point field—evolve into coherent ensembles that manifest the properties associated with life.

The level of coherence of the cluster of vibrations that create the phenomena of life is enormous. The human organisms, for example, consists of some 1,000,000 billion cells, about ten thousand times more than stars in the Milky Way galaxy. In this population of cells, 600 billion are dying, and the same number are regenerating each day—over 10 million cells per second. The average skin cell lives only for about two weeks; bone cells are renewed every three months. Every 90 seconds, millions of antibodies are synthesized, each from about 1,200 amino-acids; and every hour 200 million erythrocytes are regenerated. According to radio isotope analyses carried out at Oak Ridge Laboratories, in the span of a year 98 per cent of the atoms that make up the organism are also replaced. There is no substance in the body that would be constant during a lifetime, although heart and brain cells endure longer than most. Yet the substances that coexist at a given time produce thousands of biochemical reactions in the body each and every second.

The coordination of this vast number of cells and their complex electromagnetic and chemical signaling requires extraordinary fine-tuning among the parts: a high level of system-wide coherence. There are quasi-instant, nonlinear, heterogeneous, and multidimensional correlations among all the cells of the organism, assured by highly coordinated organs and organ systems.

This kind of order cannot arise by mechanistic interaction among individual molecules. Simple billiard-ball push-impact relations among proximal parts must be complemented by a network of instant communication that correlates all parts of the living system, even those that are distant from one another. Rare molecules, for example, are seldom contiguous, yet they find each other throughout the organism. There would not be sufficient time for this to occur by a random process of jiggling and mixing; the molecules need to locate and respond to each other specifically, even if they are distant. It turns out that the living state is dynamic and fluid, its myriad activities self-motivated, self-organizing, and spontaneous. It involves tens of thousands of genes, hundreds of thousands of proteins and other macromolecules that make up the cell, and the many kinds of cells that make up tissues and organs. There are no controlling and controlled parts or levels in this gigantic structure: all parts are in instant and continuous communication. Adjustments, responses, and changes propagate in all directions at the same time. This instant network-like correlation cannot be produced only by physical or even chemical interactions among molecules, genes, cells, and organs. Though some biochemical signaling—for example, the signaling of control genes—is remarkably effective, the speed with which activating processes spread in the body, as well as the complexity of these processes, make reliance on genetics and biochemistry alone unrealistic.

This places in question a widespread notion, still prevalent in mainstream science, that organic processes are controlled exclusively, or at least predominantly, by the organism's set of genes. It is held that the genome contains a complete set of instructions for physically and biochemically building and operating the living organism.

According to the quantum paradigm as applied to the sciences of life, this is not the case. "Genetic determinism," though a widespread doctrine, encountered two paradoxical findings. One is the "C-value paradox" (where C stands for complexity, and C-value denotes the complexity of the organism's species-specific DNA sequence) and the other is the "gene-number paradox."

The C-value paradox is created by the failure to verify that the complexity of the genome and the complexity of the organism are proportional. Yet if the genes of an organism code and control its structure and function, this should be the case. More complex organisms should have more complex genetic structures. This is not borne out by the findings. A simple amoeba turned out to have 200 times the amount of DNA in its cells than a human being. Even species that are closely related in their descent may have radically different genomes of non-corresponding size. The genome size of closely related rodents often varies by a factor of two, and the genome size of the housefly is five times larger than the genome size of the fruit fly. At the same time species of entirely different descent may have similar genetic structures. These findings are paradoxical if it is true that the structure and size of genomes determines the structure and function of the living organism.

A further paradox is created by the finding that there is a significant excess of genes in the living cell beyond those for which an organic function can be established. There are many genes of many varieties that do not have any known function. Some of them can mutate without deleterious effect on the organism, and some can mutate without any effect at all. Moreover, genes are often copied in the genome with minor modification, and this does not affect the functioning of the organism. All gene copies would have to mutate together to perturb organic function. This redundancy of genes in the cell likewise constitutes a paradox for the "gene-instruction" theory of the organism held in pre-quantum molecular biology.

The astonishingly precise, quasi-instant correlation of all the cells and cellular systems of the organism is faster and more complex than the previously known forms of correlation among the parts and elements of the organism. Living organisms are macroscopic quantum systems. Coherent multi-scale and multidimensional connections maintain the systems in their physical-biological environment and create coherence with living systems and their environment throughout the biosphere. Such constant and active interconnection is what makes the emergence and sustenance of life physically possible.

Quantum systems have remarkable properties. In such systems, a nonmaterial form of information transfer takes place using entangled states as channels of communication. Molecular reactions at distinct points in the organism carry out individual functions, but the coordination of the functions is ensured by the quantum coherence of the organism as a whole. Entangled states are nonlocal states of distant and classically noninteractive parts of the organism.

Living organisms are not skin-enclosed entities, and the living world is not the harsh domain of mainline Darwinism where each organism struggles against all others, a world with every species, every organism, and every gene competing against every other. Rather, living beings are elements in a vast network of intimate relations that embraces the biosphere—an interconnected system within the wider connections that reach out into the universe.

A macroscopic quantum system differs in essential respects from a classical system. A quantum system does not allow a precise determination of position and momentum and other non-communicating variables. There is no continuous change in energy, entropy, and information; identical parts do not have a separate identity, and there is no individual determination of the diverse attributes of the system. The quantum system allows nonclassical processes to take place, such as tunneling through potential barriers, interference among all possible histories of the communicating entities, sensitivity to electromagnetic potentials, entangled states, and teleportation. Living systems can only subsist in their intrinsically unstable state far from thermal and chemical equilibrium through constant intrinsic interconnection involving faster transmission of information than is known to mainstream science. The quantum concept of nonlocal entanglement provides an explanation of such instant multidimensional interconnection.

THE NATURE OF CONSCIOUSNESS

Classical physics maintained that all phenomena originate in the interaction of particles of matter. Everything we observe, ourselves included, is the outcome of this interaction. There is no place for mind in this world. Mind and consciousness, if not entirely illusory, are the by-product of the interaction of neurons in the brain. With modern quantum science, consciousness is finally achieving its proper place in our concept of reality: not just as a by-product, a side phenomenon of the workings of the brain, but as a principal facet of reality.

Consciousness, the new paradigm maintains, is not something unique to individuals; it is an expression of the principle of life. Consciousness expresses what is intrinsic to every cell in the body, which is the search for integration and wholeness, for cooperation and coherence. Coherence both within our inner world and our coherence outside with the outer world, where consciousness is the life principle, become manifest.

The truth of the theory that the brain produces our mind and consciousness is said to be borne out by observation. When the brain stops functioning, consciousness stops. This does not admit exceptions: a dead brain cannot produce consciousness. Phenomena of consciousness beyond the brain must be fantasy. However, it appears that on occasion consciousness is present in the absence of a living brain. The quantum paradigm offers a basis for explaining this phenomenon.

According to this paradigm, the brain is a macroscopic quantum system. Given quantum-functionality, the brain can receive information not only from the eyes and ears but from a wider world. This is possible since the brain is part of an organism, an entity that is nonlocally "entangled" with other organisms throughout the biosphere.

Insightful people, whether they are shamans or scientists, poets or prophets, have made purposive use of the nonlocal communication capacity of their brain. They are taking seriously, and making use of, the spontaneous insights emerging in their brain. And they have produced evidence for the existence of such communication. The evidence comes from a variety of sources. It comes from people who arrived at the portals of death and returned. It comes from psychic mediums who "channel" what appears to be the consciousness of people who are no longer alive. A number of such reports have been examined by scientists, medical doctors, physicists, and neurosurgeons, and most of them affirm that they are often veridical: consciousness appears to be present also beyond the brain.

Communication in the quantum universe is always two-way. There are no passive, external observers. Indeed, there is nothing in the quantum universe that would be external and passive. All elements interact with all other elements. This is the basis for the popular notion that our observations create the world. Although our observations do not create it in the usual sense, they affect the world and change it.

"Quantum brain" researchers investigate the interaction of our consciousness with the physical world, making use of advanced quantum mechanics concepts such as entanglement, phase relations, and hyperspace, among others. Investigators

in psychosomatic medicine, in particular in psychoneuroim-
munology and other forms of biofeedback research, explore the
connection between consciousness and bodily processes, while
other scientists investigate the effects of dreams, psychedelic
substances, and trance and meditative states on consciousness.
Their work recalls Einstein's insight of more than half a century
ago. "A human being" he said, "is part of the whole, called by us
'universe,' a part limited in time and space. He experiences his
thoughts and feelings as something separate from the rest—a
kind of optical delusion of his consciousness. This delusion is
a kind of prison for us, restricting us to our personal decisions
and to affection for a few persons nearest us." Leading psychologists, psychiatrists, and consciousness researchers rediscover
what ancient cultures have known: that our brain is linked by
subtle, seemingly "spiritual" connections. In the current litera-
ture, these connections are said to be "transpersonal."

The conclusion drawn from the evidence is often stated as
the affirmation that we have two modes of experiencing the
world, and not just one. One mode is the "perceptual–cognitive–
symbolic" mode, and the other the "direct–intuitive–nonlocal"
mode. The former processes signals from the physical environment, whereas the latter originates in the enfolded "implicate"
order—the Akashic dimension of the world.

The perceptual-cognitive-symbolic mode is based on the
cerebral processing of information received from the proximal
environment. This gives rise to the sights, sounds, textures, and
smells that dominate everyday consciousness. In turn, the direct-
intuitive-nonlocal mode produces subtle, seemingly spiritual

phenomena, such as visions, insights, and intuitions. These surface in dreaming, daydreaming, creative trance, mystical rapture, deep meditation, prayer, and hypnosis, as well as in conditions near the portals of death.

Since the classic studies of near-death experiences by Elisabeth Kübler-Ross, NDE have been systematically investigated by clinical psychologists and specialized researchers. It appears that people who come close to death undergo a remarkable experience that has a distinct memory component. Raymond Moody concluded that it is now "clearly established" that the experience of a significant proportion of the people who are revived following close calls with death is quite similar from case to case, regardless of the patient's age, sex, or their religious, cultural, educational or socio-economic background. NDE researcher David Lorimer investigated what he calls panoramic memory, where lived experiences resurface with remarkable speed, reality, and accuracy. The time sequence of these beyond-the-brain recollections varies: Some start in early childhood and move towards the present; others start in the present and move backwards to childhood. Still other recalls are superposed, as if in a holographic clump. Everything that a person has experienced in his or her lifetime is subject to being recalled. Nothing appears to have been permanently erased.

A related phenomenon of consciousness comes to light when psychotherapists induce a state of psychological regression in patients to recall their early childhood. Some therapists often find that they can guide patients even further back in time to the "pre-birth" experiences of being in the womb. Sometimes regression to even further back can be achieved: reaching back to experiences that seem to stem from previous lifetimes. Regressed persons tell stories of prior life experiences associated with current problems and neuroses. Psychiatrist Thorwald Dethlefsen's case histories include the story of a patient who could not see in an otherwise functional eye; he came up with the memory of living as a medieval soldier whose eye was pierced by an arrow. A patient of Morris Netherton, suffering from ulcerative colitis, relived the sensations of an eight-year-old girl shot at a mass grave by Nazi soldiers. Roger Woolger's patient, who complained of a rigid neck and shoulders, recalled an event of being a Dutch painter who committed suicide by hanging.

Reincarnation researcher Ian Stevenson found that often children recall experiences that appear to be those of living individuals. This may connect the brain and consciousness of the child with an individual who speaks a different tongue. The child begins to speak in a language he or she did not possess in the ordinary state of consciousness. The phenomenon, known as xenoglossy, cannot be explained by assuming a chance acquaintance with some elements of the given language; in several recorded cases hypnotized and regressed children engaged in prolonged and fluent conversations with native speakers in a language they did not know.

In the 1970s physicists Russell Targ and Harold Puthoff carried out some of the best-known work on telepathic thought and image transference. They wished to ascertain the reality of spontaneous signal transmission between different individuals, one of whom would act as "sender" and the other as "receiver." They placed the receiver in a sealed, opaque, and electrically shielded chamber and the sender in another room where he or she was subjected to bright flashes of light at regular intervals. Electroencephalograph (EEG) machines were used to register the brain-wave patterns of both. As expected, the sender exhibited the rhythmic brain waves that normally accompany exposure to bright flashes of light. But, after a brief interval, the receiver began to produce the same patterns, although the person was not exposed to the flashes and had not received sense-perceivable signals from the sender.

A related experiment regards the spontaneous harmonization of the brain waves of the left and right brain hemispheres of the test subject. In ordinary waking consciousness the two cerebral hemispheres—the language oriented, linearly thinking rational "left brain" and the gestalt-perceiving intuitive "right brain—manifest uncoordinated, randomly diverging patterns. Experiments show that when a subject enters a meditative state of consciousness, these patterns tend to become synchronized, and in deep meditation the two hemispheres produce nearly identical patterns. In experiments carried out in the laboratories of Cyber in Milan, when two subjects meditate at the same time, the same synchronization effect is observed not only between their individual left and right hemispheres, but also between the test subjects themselves. In pairs of deeply meditating subjects a quasi-identical four-fold synchronization emerges (left- and right-hemisphere synchronization within, as well as between the subjects), although the subjects do not see, hear, or otherwise experience each other. Such synchronization is observed in experiments with as many as twelve subjects.

Altered states seem to mediate connection between the brain and almost any part of the environing world. This conclusion has been reached by psychiatrist Stanislav Grof. He suggested that we need to add to the familiar "biographic-recollective" domain of the human psyche a "perinatal" and a "transpersonal" domain. In these domains, the individual appears capable of accessing information that is beyond the range of his or her sense organs, and may be even beyond his or her current lifetime.

Deep Insights from the East: The Wisdom of the *Dao* and the Importance of Mindful Living

It is not accidental that the core concepts of ancient Eastern thought are mirrored in, and validated by, contemporary science; particularly in the life sciences, the core concepts of Eastern thought coincide with modern science. A key element of this coincidence is the Chinese tradition's injunction to live a good life, the right way.

The traditional and now actively revived principle is that humans should live in accordance with the *Dao*, the natural force or impetus of the universe. This is mirrored in the advice we can derive from the quantum paradigm: to live in accordance with the evolutionary impetus identified as the holotropic attractor. If we live aligned with the evolutionary impetus, with the *Dao*, we thrive and flourish. And if we do not, we face growing difficulties and problems and may confront crisis and disaster.

The advice given for living a good life based on the contemporary life sciences agrees with the core concepts of the *Dao*. Not only does the holotropic attractor support the *Dao*; the quantum field of consciousness is functionally synonymous with the traditional Chinese concept of "ultimate nothingness." The traditional concepts do not provide rules for and instructions on how to live. But they do provide a philosophy for life tried and tested for thousands of years.

The coincidence of the old and the new concepts confers benefits on both. The life sciences need grounding in tried and tested wisdom, and the Eastern traditions need the authority of the life sciences to give it credence.

Traditional Chinese culture sees the universe as arising from a field of "ultimate nothingness" called the *Wuji* [2] (無極), in which the energy of the universe, the *Dao* [3] (道), creates all things, known as *Taiji* [4] (太極). All forms of matter—Taiji—have a basic binary code, a dynamic Yin-Yang (陰陽) counterpoint, like a sine wave constantly oscillating back and forth. It is within these cycles that evolution takes place and humans evolve. If humanity follows the impetus of the universe—the *Dao*— it can then create all things. If it diverges from the *Dao*, it will suffer. When aligned with the *Dao*, humanity flourishes, if not, disaster is inevitable. This idea is summed up in the Chinese concept of *xingwang* (興亡), the duality of flourishing and decay, prosperity, and death, which applies to people, societies, nations, and everything. It is the dynamic at the heart of life.

The wisdom of the East holds that the *Dao* created the Earth, and on Earth it created life, and then human life. As the Daoist canon, the *Daodejing*, puts it:[5]

> Dao gave birth to One (*Wuji*);
>
> One gave birth to Two (*Taiji* and *Yin-Yang*),
>
> Two gave birth to Three (Heaven-Earth-Humanity);
>
> Three gave birth to All Things;
>
> All Things rely on the energy of the Yin and embrace the power of the Yang,
>
> Integrating their energies to create harmony.[6]

From *Wuji* (ultimate nothingness) to *Taiji* (which means all things) to the dynamic of Yin-Yang, from the Universe to Earth and to Humanity—there is a continuous process of evolution in accordance with the *Dao*.

The creation process is described in the *Daodejing* as a process of alignment: "Humanity takes its law from the Earth; the Earth takes its law from Heaven; Heaven takes its law from the *Dao*. The law of the *Dao* is what is natural."[7]

All that humans need to do in order to live in accordance with the *Dao* is to listen to the impetus of the universe, rather than follow their desires, no matter whether these desires are right or wrong, good or bad. A key Chinese phrase is, "Do nothing and nothing will be left undone (無為而無不為),"[8] which also comes from the *Daodejing*.[9] It does not mean literally "do nothing," as is often mistakenly said, but rather it means that if people follow the flow of the universe nothing more is called for, since all will be well.

Everything can be achieved by not interfering with the *Dao*. Be one with all around you because what is good for the whole is also good for all of the parts. Don't enforce your desires and will, and you will arrive at a place where your mind is at one with the universe. Because you do what you do, and because the impetus of the universe invites you to do it, all that you create is based on the natural impetus.

A higher level of consciousness allows people to follow the *Dao*, and when they follow the *Dao*, what they are doing is not from their own will, but by the will of the *Dao*. To achieve this, humans must attain "the unity of Heaven and Humanity"—*tianrenheyi* (天人合一)—that is oneness with the universe so that they can connect to its impetus and become insightful. The result is the harmonization of relationships on all levels—with nature, with others, and with themselves—and a state of blessed well-being—*ziyouzizai* (自由自在)—that is a state of carefree living in-the-moments.

Well-being is a system-wide concept. Being well means not just the well-being of one individual, but of everything and everybody. For one to be well, ALL must be well, and for all to be well, evolution must be continuously moving in alignment with the impetus of the universe, thereby allowing for the flourishing of life. If life is flourishing, everything is aligned with the evolutionary impetus of the *Dao*.

Chinese culture, founded on the wisdom of the *Dao*, offers a practical mode for creating the next era in the history of humanity. This is an opportunity to repurpose the deep wisdom of the East for use today. The Chinese school of thought, thanks to its longevity and continuity, has grown into an all-embracing philosophy of life and relationships. It continues to be the foundation of Chinese society and offers a sound foundation for other societies as well.

We are facing monumental challenges. We need to promote the shift to the next level of consciousness so that we can respond to the challenges by achieving an understanding and appreciation of the unity of ancient wisdom and modern science— the optimal guidepost for our life and our future.

DEEP INSIGHTS FROM THE WEST: THE HOLOTROPIC ATTRACTOR AND PURPOSE IN THE UNIVERSE

The universe is more like a great thought than like a great machine. This realization, enunciated by cosmologist James Jeans over a hundred years ago, is dawning on many scientists today. It brings cosmology close to religion and spirituality and opens the way to reconsidering the idea of a divine element in nature in terms acceptable to science.

A view of the world based on quantum principles conceives of fundamental reality not as constituted of separate particles called "matter," but of interacting clusters of vibration in a universal quantum field. The coherence of the clusters indicates that they are not random, but "informed"—formed by a something that (following Max Planck, Erwin Schrödinger, David Bohm and other scientists) we can best conceive as a spirit or intelligence. It appears that there is a nonmaterial yet effective factor at work in nature. This calls to mind what the spiritual and religious doctrines call "divine." They identify it as the Divine Matrix, the Cosmic Ground, the Akashic Records, the Great Spirit, or simply The Source. In the Abrahamic religions it is the unique deity: God.

In the course of the past century, it has become clear that the universe is more than the spatial and temporal background for bits of matter moving about in passive space and indifferently flowing time. Separate, seemingly material entities appear only on the surface. Below or beyond the universe's manifest dimension there is an interconnected domain that is not material, but energetic and "informed." The quantum field is not passive and unchanging; it is dynamic and interconnected. The universe is a dynamic matrix that "in-forms" the events that appear on its surface. The deep dimension—called "implicate order" by David Bohm—is not observable in itself, but its effect are observable. They are revealed by hypotheses applied to otherwise inexplicable phenomena in the surface "explicate order."

The conception of a deep dimension that would lie somewhere below or beyond the observed world is as old as systematic philosophy, but it is relatively new in science. Until recently, mainstream scientists refused to concede that an immaterial factor, conceivably originating in another dimension would influence events in the observable world. They held that today's remarkable coherent universe is the outcome of chance inter- actions occurring over a sufficiently extended period of time. Given enough time, they said, even Shakespeare's Hamlet will appear when a monkey keeps hitting the keys of a typewriter.

Not only the evolution of the universe, but also the evolu- tion of life was denied connection with nonmaterial factors. The products of evolution, it was said, are the outcome of chance interactions subject to random and in the long-term productive iteration as an extended series of trials and errors. Darwin, and more than Darwin himself, his followers, suggested that every- thing we find in nature is the product of blind and purpose- less interactions.

The way things are can be fully explained by genetic muta- tions subjected to natural selection. According to Oxford biolo- gist Richard Dawkins, the living world may give the impression of having been designed for a purpose, but this is not the case. Cheetahs, for example, give every indication of having been designed to kill antelopes. The teeth, claws, eyes, nose, leg muscles, and brain of a cheetah are precisely what we would expect if nature's purpose in creating cheetahs was to maxi- mize deaths among antelopes. At the same time, antelopes are fast, agile and watchful, they seem to be designed to escape cheetahs. The existence of such species need not be ascribed to a higher design; they can be explained in reference to "utility functions." Cheetahs have the utility function to kill antelopes, and antelopes have the utility function to escape cheetahs.

Nature is indifferent as to whether or not they succeed. The properties of species are precisely the properties that would appear if there was no purpose and no good in nature, only blind and pitiless indifference. Evidently, a blind and pitiless world contradicts the existence of a purposeful and benevolent factor, such as a God or some other higher spirit.

This, however, proved to be a mistaken assumption. Calculations based on observations and now carried out by powerful programs show that chance events are extremely unlikely to have produced the observed universe in the available timeframe. 13.8 billion years since the big bang is far too short to explain the formation of the genetic pool even of a fruit-fly by a random mixing of genes. A factor we have called "directional information" must be biasing the unfolding of otherwise random interactions. This factor works like an "attractor" in a complex system: it influences the unfolding of chance interactions in a determinable direction. This is the direction observations show underlie the partially nondeterminate but on the whole nonchaotic processes of physical, chemical, and biological evolution.

The long-term unfolding of evolutionary processes is a canonical trend. It takes off from the initial chaos that characterized the state of the universe following the big bang, and encompasses the order exhibited by the evolution of stars, stellar systems and galaxies, as well as the amazingly precise, complex and coherent order that came about on Earth and conceivably on myriad other planets. As a result, we live in a complex and coherent universe, and are complex and coherent macroscopic quantum systems ourselves: systems of quanta integrated in complex and coherent chains of molecules integrated in complex and coherent cells and cellular systems.

The nonmaterial factor functioning as an attractor in the universe is "holotropic": it provides directional information a definite, statistically revealed direction. This changes the universe from a world of random interaction into a world of statistically revealed but overall consistent evolution.

In the context of science, we need to add an important lemma. The holotropic attractor is not (or not necessarily, for agnosticism is the reasonable position and not atheism) the manifestation of a transcendent entity. It is not (or not necessarily) beyond the bounds of space and time. It is not likely to act "on" the observable world, and is not likely even to be a "part of" the observable world. The attractor *is* the world. The universe is simply such that it acts as an attractor for the events that emerge in it. As the integral cosmic "whole-system" it is the source of the bias that favors the emergence of complex and coherent systems in a sea of otherwise random interaction.

The universe is holotropic. Why so? This is a reasonable query, but it is beyond the ken of empirical science. The transcendental stream of religious and spiritual traditions tells us more. It tells us that the universe is the product of a Creator: a Cosmic Mind or Consciousness, and this nonmaterial agency is beyond space and time. We could specify that this agency could be the source of the holotropism of the universe. This proposition is reasonable, but it is not verifiable by natural science. Evidence for it must lie in the province of mystical intuition, rather than protocolled observation.

The more modest science-based affirmation is that the logically implied nonmaterial agency is not in the universe and is not acting *on* the universe—it *is* the universe. This is a daring but cogent hypothesis. It accounts for the emergence of life as a natural, and not as a predominantly chance process. And it affirms that there is purpose underlying evolution in the universe, including the evolution of life.

PART TWO

Western and Eastern Approaches to an Era of Well-Being

CHAPTER 3

The Western
Science-Based Approach

GUIDANCE FROM THE QUANTUM PARADIGM

In the mainstream of Western civilization, science enjoys unrivalled authority. Science, however, is not a static phenomenon: it changes and evolves. At its leading edge new paradigms are arising. The paradigm coming to light today is based on the natural sciences, more particularly, on the quantum sciences: quantum physics, cosmology, biology, and even quantum consciousness research. The currently arising new paradigm is a quantum paradigm.

A key message of the emerging paradigm is that the universe itself evolves; its laws are constant, but the phenomena to which they apply are not. The entities of the physical world are quantum entities: clusters and superclusters of coherent vibration. They change and evolve in a coherent way, and the direction toward which they evolve is not only coherent in the sense of being comprehensible—they are coherent in themselves. Coherence, created by the subtle but effective action of the orientation of the evolutionary process, is the focal point, and possibly the ultimate end, of the evolution we see in the universe. It is the overall direction of change in the plethora of systems that arise and continue to emerge in space and time.

As noted, the basic orientation of the evolutionary processes is accounted for by the holotropic attractor. This attractor accounts for the dynamic impulse that created the universe from the initial post-big bang chaos, and continues to create the universe through the myriad systems that had emerged since then. Here on Earth, the holotropic attractor determines the orientation of the evolutionary processes that govern change in the manifold physical, physio-chemical, biological, and eco-social systems that populate this planet.

The essence of these processes is orientation toward coherence in whole-system entities. This orientation provides guidance for our thinking and behavior. It gives us information on our alignment, or lack of alignment, with the evolutionary processes of the universe. Alignment with these processes is a natural condition, a condition of health and well-being; it signifies our connection with the source. It is the gist of the message of the world's great religions and spiritual systems. In popular vernacular, it means "going with the force," the power of the energy in the universe. It is to recognize and to respect that in the natural world the coherent wholeness of every entity is its decisive characteristic. Well-being arises by a system's alignment with the holotropic attractor—and thus "going with the force." Hence the meaning of the greeting "May the force be with you."

Alignment with the attractor—with the evolutionary impulse in the universe—calls for cooperation: working together to maintain the coherence of the whole. Darwin saw competition as the fundamental principle of survival in the living world; he referred to it as "the survival of the fittest." However, as researchers in the new biology and psychology recognize, a higher motivation than competition is present both in the human body and in the human psyche. That motivation is a tropism toward cooperation: toward finding and promoting unity and wholeness.

THE QUANTUM PARADIGM IN SOCIETY

Coherence in society calls for working together and creating the system where "I" becomes "WE"—where the parts maintain their unique identity while working together to maintain the integral coherence of the whole that they form. This is the principle we obtain from the quantum paradigm. Public policy is the field for the application of this principle. It defines the coexistence of unique but not separate individuals in coherent wholes, whether these wholes are states and nations, or businesses or social and cultural groups.

The operative principle of alignment can be stated in reference to the perennial question of desirability in the governance of life in society. This "wholeness principle" can be encapsulated in a single phrase. *What is good for the whole is good for the part.* In the context of human society, the whole is the web of life in the biosphere, and the part is an individual entity—a human being, a family or tribe, a community, or a business enterprise.

The wholeness principle has been applied in traditional societies where the whole included humans, their families and societies, as well as their natural environment. However, the principle has been neglected in the modern world. In fact, the modern world has been operating on the basis of the opposite and contrary principle: *what is good for the part* (that is, for me and whatever I regard as belonging to me) *is* [or is likely to be] *good for the whole* (which is everybody and everything else). If this currently dominant principle for the organization of life in society were true, we would not need to worry about anybody else, whether person, community, business, or the environment; we could pursue our own interests free of moral and intellectual commitment to the good of everybody else.

The organization of life in society on the basis of the currently operative principle is counter-functional: it produces strongly negative results. The fact is that what is immediately good for the part—for me, my tribe or family, my community and my business—may not prove to be good for the whole, which is the web of life on the planet. My "good" could deprive others from having needed resources, such as living spaces and positive relations among themselves and with the rest of the biosphere. In the long-term, the good of the part coincides with the good of the whole, but in the short-term it may not do so— and then the long-term may not be reached without encountering major and possibly fatal problems.

The "unholy" operative principle, when practiced by the economic and political centers of power, tends to lead to unfair and unsustainable conditions in society. It produces conflict, resistance, and revolt and leads to catastrophic consequences for the centers of power themselves. This has been amply demonstrated in the annals of history. It has led to WWII, through Nazi Germany's adherence to the "part comes first" principle expressed in the slogan *Deutschland ueber Alles* (Germany above all). Pursuing the interests of Nazi Germany above all others was not good for the "*Alles*" (for the rest of the world), given that the rest of the world was—or would have been—subjugated to the Nazi ideology. But the Nazi regime collapsed, as acting on the unholy principle has led to its defeat. And that was not good for Germany either.

In today's world, this very same unholy principle was proclaimed by Donald Trump. He declared "America First" and concentrated on "making America great again." Acting on this principle, Trump withdrew the United States from the Paris Agreement on Climate Change, refused multilateral cooperation with its partners in North America, engaged in a trade war with China, and stopped support for the World Health Organization even though it was combating the Corona-19 virus pandemic, which was in the interest of the American people themselves. Fortunately, the Biden administration is rectifying many of these mistaken measures.

We live in an integral quantum universe and not in a mechanistic world where whole and parts are separate, or even separable. In the intrinsically whole quantum universe, the whole is the existential context for the existence of the parts. Not only in abstract theory, but also in concrete practice, the whole and the part need to be treated as one, and for the good of the part, the whole needs to receive priority attention.

The wholeness principle applies to the organization of human life today, and will apply to it tomorrow. If any part— meaning any individual, community, business, nation, or ethnic or cultural group—fails to benefit from the good of the whole, it is not because what is good for it as a part would be different from what is good for the whole, but because the whole is not well structured; it is deficient. The way to remedy this deficiency is not by putting the part above the whole, as most contemporary politicians and business executives do. It is by shaping the whole so that it allows access to resources and benefits for all. This calls for shaping public policy in accordance with the operative principle of societal organization. The integrity of the whole of human society defines the good for all, including the good of all the states, nations and communities that exist in the world today—and, unless a global catastrophe intervenes, will continue to exist tomorrow.

THE QUANTUM PARADIGM IN LEADERSHIP

Searching for the creation of an era of well-being places major responsibilities on the shoulders of political as well as business leadership. The quality of leaders is essential in any process of transition, most of all in society's emergence from a global crisis. Leaders acting according to the model of the quantum paradigm need to be aware of the wholeness principle in society. They are agents of the evolution of human life and should endeavor to guide this evolution toward higher levels of cooperation with the living systems that populate the biosphere. There is nothing more important in any group and in any society than having an informed and responsible leader. The quantum leader—the leader acting on the wholeness principle deriving from the quantum paradigm—is one who focuses on aligning, collaborating, and creating conditions conducive to the flourishing of life.

The science of seeds created the agrarian era, and the science of Newtonian physics and engineering created the industrial era, both of which centered on raising economic production. But economic production is not the panacea for confronting the challenges of our time. Even the term "economic" is being redefined. It is increasingly considered in terms of the challenges of sustainability and related to the objective of achieving a higher level of well-being in society.

The quantum-paradigm leader is not a super businessman or businesswoman uniquely dedicated to the growth of the economy. The process of radically refining what we are and what we understand as change for the good of society is now underway. The United Nations has led the way with its call in 2012 to consider well-being and happiness as a new economic paradigm, leading to the milestone "Sustainability Mandate" in 2015. This has led to the spread of conscious capitalism and the declaration of this name in 2019 by the Business Roundtable, a grouping of major US companies. The Declaration called on commercial enterprises to serve interests wider than those of their shareholders: "While each of our individual companies serves its own corporate purpose, we share a fundamental commitment to all of our stakeholders. We commit to: delivering value to our customers . . . investing in our employees . . . dealing fairly and ethically with our suppliers (and) supporting the communities in which we work. We respect the people in our communities and protect the environment by embracing sustainable practices across our businesses."[10]

Through the overall economic growth achieved in the past three decades, humanity has exploited nearly all the economically accessible energy and material resources of the planet. The focus of economics now needs to shift to sustainability and the distribution of the benefits of a sustainable society. These are the objectives that await implementation by quantum-paradigm leaders. They need to be well prepared, not just with the tools for increasing economic and industrial production, but with the wisdom to render these benefits widely accessible and make the process itself sustainable. Quantum leaders need to embrace the wholeness principle in business as well as in society.

Quantum leaders lead by identifying movements of advanced thinking that will benefit society and our Earth. They have a keen eye and the sensitivity to resonate with trends that advance the development of economic, business, and sociocultural movements. Solutions to environmental issues are no longer peripheral but central to the objectives of the new leaders. They realize that human populations and the natural environment are not separate and separable: they form one integral system.

The leader effectively serving the good of society serves the interest of all life on the planet. This requirement may appear idealistic and even utopian in the context of today's dominant ideology in business and politics. But the post-pandemic era requires radical changes in our idea and ideals of leadership. The quantum paradigm offers the necessary fundamental reorientation.

CHAPTER 4

The Chinese Tradition-Based Approach

Our culture is created from our worldview, how we see the world and the way in which we choose to live. The principle at the heart of Chinese thought is that humans should live and create in accordance with the natural forces of the universe. If they do, the sages say, they thrive and flourish. If they do not, they face decay and disaster.

A new worldview and a new approach to relating to each other is required. The traditional wisdom of life expressed in Eastern culture in general, and in the Chinese cultural tradition in particular, is a precious guide for finding the path to an era of well-being.

FOUR FUNDAMENTAL QUESTIONS ACCORDING TO THE TRADITIONS OF CHINA

In the traditional Chinese worldview, the fundamental questions we ask define who we are. The following questions are decisive: We seek knowledge about what life is and question the purpose of our life; we ask what is well-being, and in the language of ancient Chinese traditions we seek "the medicine of life" for answers about illness and healing. These are also the questions we examined in chapter one as fundamental for the contemporary era as well.

1. What Is Life?

The Yellow Emperor's Inner Canon

The answer to the first of four fundamental questions in the optic of Chinese wisdom defines life as an expression of nature. When we observe nature, we know that life is nature, and well-being is essential aspiration of life itself.

One of the most important of the books at the heart of Chinese culture, *The Yellow Emperor's Inner Canon—huangdineijing* (黃帝內經),[11] dating 2,200 years ago, describes the power of humanity to guide the process of creation. It categorically places the human species at the apex of life:

> Among all things in Heaven and Earth,
> Nothing is more precious than Humanity.
> Humanity is born from the Qi of Heaven and Earth
> And nurtured through the Four Seasons.[12]

The *Daodejing* also stresses the special place accorded to humanity in the greater scheme of things, thereby recognizing that the well-being of humanity is crucial to the harmony of the entire system:

The *Dao* is great, Heaven is great,
Earth is great and Humanity is also great.[13]

In the Chinese worldview, there are four "greats" in the universe, and humanity is one of them. Humanity is great because it participates in creation. The universe created life, and humans are the most valuable life form of the universe at the forefront of the evolutionary chain. With their consciousness, humans actively participate in the creation of life. The choices they make are a dance with the *Dao*, an expression of the *Dao* in creation and in collective consciousness. To be in line with the *Dao*, people must choose wisely and learn how to live according to the *Dao*. If they do, they live to an old age in good health.

The Yellow Emperor's Inner Canon offers a blueprint for life with its description of the chain that links the whole universe, even to the smallest element of life:

Heaven within us is Virtue (*de* 德).

Earth within us is Qi (*qi* 气).

The flow of Virtue and Qi produces Life (者).

From Life comes the Essence (of Yin-Yang).

The Essence (*jing* 精) of the two (Yin and Yang) intersect to form Divinity (*shen* 神).

What accompanies Divinity as it moves in and out is called Spirit (*hun* 魂).

What accompanies the movement of Essence in and out is called Soul (*po* 魄).

What commands all existence is the Heart (*xin* 心).

The memory of the Heart is Consciousness (*yi* 意).

What remains in Consciousness is Will (*zhi* 志).

What fluctuates depending on Will is Thought (*si* 思).

What is seen from a distance due to Thought is Consideration (*lu* 慮).

Dealing with matters with due Consideration is Wisdom (*zhi* 智).[14]

In this way, *The Yellow Emperor's Inner Canon* states that life is a consequence of the interaction of the energies of Heaven and Earth, Yin and Yang. These two energies are dancing with each other in a process of integration, and the resulting energy is the human spirit, *Shen* (神). The universe provides human beings with their basic nature, which is virtue—in Chinese *de* (德) is the expression of the *Dao* in human nature, and it is nurtured by *Qi* (氣) from the Earth. So the essence of the building-material of life is *Jing* (精), *Qi* (氣), the nurturing energy from Heaven and Earth, and *Shen* (神), the human spirit. These three words are united in a famous phrase—*Jing-Qi-Shen* (精氣神)— essence, energy, and spirit combined. That is human life. The dance of the two forms of energy (from Heaven and from Earth) is divinity.

Another section of *The Yellow Emperor's Inner Canon* talks about *Po* (魄)—the human soul—and about mind, which is what creates and manages external reality. The Canon also talks about thoughts, *Si* (思), which what people use to analyze and make sense of the world, and tells us about *Lei* (累), the accumulation of thoughts that create *Yi* (意), experiential accumulation. Finally there is *Zhi* (志), which is willpower, an expression of the subconscious.

As to the human body, the traditional Chinese view is that the body is made up of five elements: water, wood, metal, fire, and earth (水木金火土).[15] This can be understood to mean, for instance, that sun and water give birth to plants, which give rise to other forms of life, and whatever we eat is converted back into water and earth. We now know that our bodies are composed of up to sixty percent water plus a variety of minerals, and through the process of digestion what we eat becomes part of our body. The body is a highly sophisticated system capable of producing a wide range of chemicals and biochemicals, thereby allowing it to repair many of its ills.

The quantum paradigm's view of human life, paralleling the Chinese view, is that the living human body is both a coherent system of in-phase vibrations acting as part of the wider evolution of the universe, and also a unit of consciousness, the result of the integration of all the perceptions accessed in the course of an individual's evolution.

2. What Is Life's Purpose?

The *Dao*

For thousands of years, the fundamental concept of Chinese thought has been that the purpose of life is to propagate life and to strive for alignment with the universe. Life is created and can flourish when we follow our true nature, which is to follow the impetus of the universe. The evolutionary energy of the *Dao* known as *Qi* orients us in the creation of life and in the flourishing of life in accordance with our nature, and in accordance with the *Dao*. Everything works together, moving towards the flourishing of life in a natural cooperation.[16] This is especially true of humans because they are at the forefront of consciousness and evolution.

If a person understands the *Dao*, he or she is united with the source and is a free spirit. Such a person does not follow anybody, heeds only his/her own nature in alignment with the *Dao* and creates in coherence with the *Dao*. He/she also has a sense of future trends. To predict the future, to create in the midst of oneness, and to live in a state of freedom, requires wisdom. When wisdom is attained, people can create and follow their life's purpose.

Thus the purpose of life is to propagate life to enable the bio-social systems in which humanity is embedded to flourish. Human beings are to align with the natural state of flow—i.e., "do nothing and all will be done"—and live naturally and in harmony with other forms of life. The purpose of life is to be in sync with the evolutionary energy of the universe. When that is achieved, human beings reach a state of well-being.

Humanity is evolving from the trillions of cells of which each human body is composed. Some of these cells are formed into a new entity, a biosocial and ecological system of collective consciousness propagating as a discrete organism constituted by more than seven billion people. This organism needs to function well to be coherent, because if it is not coherent, it is not well. Coherence of mind-body-spirit with the *Dao* is the key measure of well-being both for individual humans and for the wider entity we know as humanity.

3. What is Well-Being?

The Chinese Philosophical System

The concept of well-being is important because well-being is the goal for individuals and for other entities both great and small. Well-being is a whole system because life is a whole system—life is everything, and everything is life, so humanity can only be well if all is well. The conclusions derived from the Chinese tradition fully coincide with the wholeness principle flowing from the paradigm of contemporary science.

In terms of the Chinese philosophy, well-being is when every system is seamlessly and naturally calibrating and creating a state in which everything is well. The word "well-being" can be rendered in Chinese as *ziyouzizai* (自由自在), meaning a state of being that is "care-free and in-the-moment"—in this state there is no resistance; one is totally open, in the way of a newborn child. To achieve this state, humans need to unite themselves with the universe. When they do, they are "blessed"—the Chinese word for that is *xingfu* (幸福).

The goal of all human beings is to lead a blessed and care-free life. Well-being means having achieved this goal through a process of awakening our awareness to a state of cooperation and creativity and a desire to align with that which is necessary for living a good life. Humans need to allow the impulse of the universe to flow through them to manifest itself as creativity and motivation to be in alignment with the state of well-being. Well-being is a whole-system condition because no individual can be well unless the whole system is well. When people are awakened and aware, they are aligned with the *Dao* and aligned to each other. Just as the bees are aligned with the birds, humanity is aligned with the *Dao* and creates life through cooperation, adjusting to each other's movements in a seamless and natural way.

Well-being and wellness, it should be noted, are not the same. "Well-being" is an aspirational state of life, while "wellness" refers to the interventions humans perform on themselves to improve their health. Our state of living is not always well, and sometimes there is a need for measures that bring us closer to alignment with the universe. A blessed life is achieved by following the *Dao*, achieving unification, and the result is authentic living with joy.

Wellness is an important part of well-being in both the body and mind. The opposite of wellness is sickness, which is defined by ancient Chinese thought, the same as in Buddhist teachings, as a condition of ignorance. The *Daodejing* addresses the difference between well-being and sickness in this way:

> To know what you don't know, is best.
> To not know, but believe yourself to know, is to have sickness.
> Sages do not become sick because they know what sickness is and so avoid it.

Treating sickness as sickness is the only way to avoid sickness.[17]

In other words, the origin of sickness is ignorance, and by knowing, sickness can be avoided. If you don't know and you know that you don't know, that is all right; but if you don't know and yet claim that you do—which is very widespread in the world—then you are sick. That is why it is said that because sages know the symptoms of sickness, and because they are vigilant and treat the symptoms of their sickness, they do not really get sick. (The same concept occurs in the teachings of the Buddha: If you know everything, how would you get sick?)

4. What is the Medicine of Life?

The "medicine of life" is a journey of awakening because we are ignorant and need to wake from our ignorance. More specifically, the medicine of life is any action or intervention by human beings that enhances our alignment with the *Dao*, the energy of the universe.

To understand the medicine of life, it is necessary to first understand the origin of all sickness. The medicine of life keeps human beings on the path of alignment, on the path to be natural and authentic and to listen, to cultivate, and to awaken. And from a new awareness, they cooperate and create. Taking a holistic approach to medicine and healing allows humanity to escape the forces distancing people from alignment towards decay and destruction.

Traditional Chinese culture views human beings as the result of the integration of the energy of the universe and the energy of the earth, the material essence containing a soul and a consciousness. Consciousness is the emperor of all things because it creates the body and is in charge of it. In the vision of Chinese culture, the *Qi* from heaven and from Earth meet and combine to create life. The aspiration of life is to flourish and to create. Human beings are units of consciousness spun off from the universe oriented toward well-being.

The Yellow Emperor's Inner Canon includes a detailed explanation of how the body is divided into twelve different departments and what each department does.[18] It is like a system of ministries in a governmental structure with consciousness controlling all. Consciousness monitors the various parts of the human operating system in a way we could call guidance and functional medicine. To maintain good health all movements should be in line with the structure of the universe, laid out in terms of twenty-four fifteen-day periods (*Jieqi,* 節氣) and five directions (*Fangwei,* 方位).[19] These provide the coordinates in time and space for living in alignment and with contentment. This is identified as the state of well-being, rooted in the great moral virtues of life.

As stated, the human body is the most sophisticated factory of medicaments known to humankind. Every medicinal remedy ever manufactured can also be produced by our body. Our body has the capacity to heal itself, but when our body is out of balance with the natural world there is an information mismatch that causes the failure of the body to produce the needed medicaments. When information flows correctly, the body self-balances and heals. This is the natural movement of the *Dao* for growth and flourishing. Ignorance is the root of all sickness. Well-being starts with wellness and the application of the medicine of life.

THE JOURNEY OF LIFE

The Confucian System of Relational Ethics: The Great Learning

Our life journey toward achieving the "good" in the Chinese tradition is framed by the Confucian system of relational ethics. This is the system in which the Daoist elements of longevity, freedom, and health are integrated with the Buddhist elements of eternal happiness and the ending of suffering. In collective terms the goal of the journey is the creation of a community of humanity, the Great Unity, while the individual's path is to reach the highest expression of creativity to fulfill our potential for health in a holistic way. The Chinese medicine of life paradigm is a combination of three systems of belief and thought: Confucian, Daoist, and Buddhist. The life journeys are governed by these ways of thinking that are tightly integrated with each other. They are unified within the fluctuating Yin-Yang cycles of energy, which is the *Dao*, and are the foundation of the ethical system at the base of Chinese society today.

The basic purpose of the journey of life is the aspiration to attain "oneness with the universe," *tianrenheyi* (天人合一).[20] In other words, this purpose is alignment with the *Dao*. To achieve this is to find harmony within ourselves, with others, and with the universe.

How do we achieve this objective? Everything starts with the individual and a shift in his or her own consciousness. As described earlier, the *Daodejing* offers a hierarchical chain of human states of mind and asks that human beings strive to embrace the highest level, the *Dao*. In the process of a constant calibration of the universe, there are opportunities to find new avenues and means for shifting consciousness. People can enter new states of consciousness for healing, but ironically it is only with fundamental disruption and chaos that truly new systems can be created. Humanity evolves through challenges, and the more chaotic the challenge, the bigger the shift in consciousness that it catalyzes.

When any of the three kinds of relationship—with self, with others, and with the environment—are unwell, connections are lost and chaos emerges. Rebuilding fundamental relationships is the only way toward well-being. In particular, when the internal relationship with self is harmonized, our relationship with others and with the environment will change. Change yourself and the world will change around you. As the *Daodejing* says, follow the *Dao* and prosper, go against the *Dao* and face destruction. The concept of Great Unity, *datong* (大同),[21] based on the concept of "harmony in diversity," *he'erbutong* (和而不同), is a social view of humanity reflecting the reality of nature, and how different things—the birds and the bees, the flowers and the trees—are all different, yet everything harmonizes and collaborates in the natural movement of life's creation process. This is unity in diversity. The *Dao* will create a new iteration of the universe, and how humans participate and how much pain they need to endure to achieve alignment is their choice.

Confucian ethics provides a framework for the journey of life and the relationships that compose our experience. Following these ethics for living has been proven effective for millennia. It is thought that an individual cannot be well until the system is well, and the system will not be well until all relationships are well. Handling these relationships is the essence of Confucian ethics, as laid out in one of the Confucian classics called *The Great Learning*—Daxue (大學)—a guide to the journey and a model for reconnection during global chaos.[22]

Confucius lived about 2,500 years ago. His classic guide for those who aspire to achieve wholeness within the Confucian relational framework was chosen during the Song Dynasty around 1,000 years ago as the basis of the Imperial Examination system. It became the foundation for the Chinese state and Chinese society that have both existed with a remarkable degree of consistency ever since.

Before the modern era, educated Chinese people were encouraged to study this book when they reached the age of fifteen because its contents were considered to be what every adult should know. Education in the traditional Chinese system up to the age of twelve involved accumulating knowledge and reciting the classics. At around twelve years old, students began to travel with their teacher to experience different places.

But by the age of fifteen, students were considered adults, and the focus shifted to learning how to manage relationships and life-relational ethics.

The Great Learning lays out all the human relationships and how human beings should live life according to the framing of these. The purpose of the book, we are told, is to allow people to create according to the virtue provided to them by the universe. This is human nature—innately virtuous—and using that gift allows creation with renewal of creativity every day. Healthy relationships strengthen connections and collective cohesiveness. The goal of *The Great Learning* is laid out in its opening sentence:

> The path to great learning
>
> Consists of manifesting shining virtue
>
> Being benevolent to the people
>
> And settling for nothing less than absolute goodness.[23]

The purpose of *The Great Learning* is to develop this "goodness"—*shan* (善). It is measured in terms of wholeness. The more holistic our choices, decisions, and intentions are, the better off people are will be because well-being is a function of the whole system. The concept of goodness extends from the individual all the way to the universe. For the individual, the goal is alignment with the essence of the universe, so that our consciousness and our willpower are oriented in the right way. Then begins the journey of self-cultivation in the context of family and country and everything under the heaven. Beyond the individual, the concept of goodness extends to the universe and to the concept of "Great Unity," a utopian vision of the world in which everything is at peace, and all elements thrive together in harmony. This is the foundation of Confucian relational ethics.

The Great Learning is important in understanding the foundations of the relationships that are essential to life. These concepts remain a fundamental influence today in Chinese culture in regard to ethics and creativity. *The Great Learning* of Confucius can be used as the framework that embraces the basic forms of wisdom, including the Buddhist Eightfold Path and the philosophy of the *Dao*. All are applicable within the framework of the Confucian ethical system of relational wellness to be achieved by self-cultivation, humility, respect for life-learning, and acting with virtue to create wholeness. This enables the practice of creating positive relationships, freeing oneself of ignorance, and choosing wisely by following one's inherent nature.

The *I Ching* (*The Book of Changes*)

The *I Ching*,[24] known in English as *The Book of Changes,* also has great value in navigating the journey of life. The book analyses positive and negative influences on life—the twin concepts of *xiong* (凶) and *ji* (吉), negative and positive, malignant and auspicious. They are considered in a matrix which is, in effect, a mathematical model mirroring the interaction of the energy from three sources: the Universe, Earth, and Humanity. The *I Ching* provides a strategy for altering a person's life and as a consequence change his or her providence. This can be done with a shift in consciousness that makes it possible to see things more clearly. Those who do this will have a blessed life, one that is joyous and contented. The Chinese concept of "blessed," *xingfu* (幸福) is that what every human being on the face of the planet wants to have: a blessed life. The more a person moves with the *Dao*, the more blessed he or she will be. Embarking on the journey of life in the direction of the *Dao* starts with the process of self-cultivation towards well-being, and this produces awakening. And awakening brings the blessedness referred to in the *I Ching* within one's grasp.

The wisdom needed to fulfill the purpose of life is addressed in a passage in the *I Ching* that discusses what it is to be blessed: [25]

> The first dimension makes it possible to see the future and predict it, which is to be blessed.
>
> The second dimension makes it possible to identify with the source, oneness, which is to be blessed.[26]
>
> The third dimension is the freedom to live in a state of well-being, which is to be blessed.[27]

Being blessed, it can be said, is synonymous with being fortunate, and in Chinese the word for good fortune is *ji* (吉). The three dimensions of being blessed referred to in the *I Ching* form the way of mindful living.

The three books, *The Yellow Emperor's Inner Canon*, *The Great Learning*, and the *I Ching*, along with the Buddhist *Heart*

Sutra comprise a comprehensive set of wisdom practices to live a life of freedom and joy in unity. Embracing this attitude, and acknowledging our virtues, is a revelation. The core requirements are awakening, alignment, cooperation, and creation. Chinese people are taught they must remember that they create from their innate virtues, from their authentic nature. If they do, they reach goodness and wholeness. As the Chinese phrase puts it, "If I am good and you are good and we are all good, then everything is good." If decisions are made based for the good of all, value is then added to the process of evolution. That is goodness.

The Great Learning says the following on the topic of developing wisdom to govern the relational ethics of our lives:

> Develop wisdom, the wisdom of observing the material world to understand its essence and how things work, and also the wisdom of the spiritual world of unity inside us, through stillness. When we develop this system of internal reality, and with determination, our mind moves to the right place, and we start living our life in the right way. Then we go through a process of development, first our own self, then family, then country, and finally all of creation—peace under heaven.[28]

There is a process, a journey of exploration, to a place of truth where individuals have self-mastery and manage everything around them in a holistic way. The result is the utopia of the "Great Unity," peace on Earth, and the flourishing of life.

Life is a journey of evolution, and the purpose of life is creating life itself. Well-being means oneness, freedom, and being in-the-moment, and the reward for embracing the approach to well-being is a life of joy.

THE SIGNIFICANCE OF
CHINESE TRADITIONS TODAY

As we look toward the advent of the era of well-being, the exploration of Eastern wisdom traditions, and more specifically the Chinese wisdom tradition, can take us to the next level of evolutionary possibilities. The Chinese worldview, with roots that go far back with unmatched continuity, is an infrastructure of great relevance for our future. In this respect, it is important to highlight that it is the ancient esoteric wisdom and cultural practices that are the focus of this discussion, not the economic or political status of contemporary China or any of its current entailments and implications.

At the dawn of a new era, human beings need to change the way they live and become more mindful of life and life's journey. Everything needs to be rethought, and our basic life systems must be reconstructed independently of the construct of the world as it currently exists. There will be a great shift from the era of the First Scientific Revolution defined by the materialistic ideas of people such as Isaac Newton and Adam Smith to the Second Scientific Revolution defined by the life sciences of consciousness and by the vastly greater use of technology in our lives. This will completely transform the way human beings live, breaking global boundaries of space and time and moving humanity speedily towards the goal of oneness and holism.

The universe is constantly calibrating with itself and its systems, reflecting collaboration in diversity. This is a dynamic process of alignment with its elements to arrive at harmonic balance. We need to awaken to the deep truth of this arrangement, and we can do so because we are creative. At its core, humanity cannot go against nature. There is a need to awaken to the fact that all things in the natural world are continually aligning and realigning with each other, collaborating in natural movement as the elements work toward their flourishing.

Contemporary scientists researching the quantum paradigm continually prove the truth of this statement. A more holistic and less conflicted approach is emerging in science, a science that is more capable than ever of integrating mindful living and finding purpose and well-being into the framing of life. The Chinese traditionally believe success is the result of a confluence of space, time, and human collaboration with Earth's other beings—a harmony of all the core elements. That is also the quantum paradigm. The timing is right for an awakening. Human beings are ready for a new global phase in which humanity has the opportunity to create the Great Unity. To do this, there is a need to elevate consciousness to a level where all can see our true nature and to allow it to guide our relationships, thereby freeing us to evolve naturally and create new living systems. In the new era, a new education system is needed that prepares people to live life in alignment with the universe and nature. There is also a need for a new approach to the liberal arts which focuses on the journey of life, just as the Confucian classic, *The Great Learning*, does.

The goal is to achieve harmony and unity amidst diversity to make human society a reflection of the reality of nature. By integrating the Western life science of consciousness with traditional Chinese wisdom a foundational structure for universal ethics will guide humankind's journey toward Great Unity, a society in which diversity is not only respected but deployed in the process of creation and collaboration. It is only in diversity that great things are made. The same things brought together create more of the same things, but diversity creates something extraordinary.

The future will surely be that more and more people awaken to this insight and embrace a purposeful life in a community of oneness. The future will be different because people will live differently; they will be enabled by technology enhancement to live closer to nature. People will have the choice of being close to their families and the community where they live and will integrate work and learning into life more organically. The foundations of economics will change because economics is about activity to meet human desires, and those desires are going to change as the focus of life shifts to our wellbeing. With the help of technology, the urban planning and entire rural-urban relationship can change, too, as more effective distribution systems are created. People are now viewing things more holistically. For instance, as the Dutch historian Rutger Bergman discusses in his book *Utopia for Realists*,[29] there is a growing realization that economic models must change from being based on per capita income and GDP growth to well-being and happiness. In this new scenario, there is no room for consumerism, at least not in its current form in which people are purposively motivated to consume.

An important element of Chinese traditional thought is the idea of "no waste." Don't waste nature, don't waste anything, and embrace recycling as one of the most important economic activities. Today, people are too wasteful, and that impacts on economics as well. Those who spend more than they make will become poor, but those who make more than they spend will accumulate wealth. It is a very simple principle; yet today the system promotes credit, encouraging the spending of future wealth. To be respectful of resources is part of mindful living in accordance with nature, where the systems are always calibrating and recalibrating into a balance.

The techno-industrial system already produces more than enough of everything to support every person on the planet. What is lacking is a holistic worldview to provide us with a new understanding of the purpose of life and of the methods which can heal our body and mind to accomplish well-being. This may sound like a pipe dream, but it is totally achievable with new technology. Humanity has always oscillated between shortage and abundance, but as long as it awakens to holism, new technology will enable adjustments to rebalance quickly.

When needs change, everything else changes, too, including the economic, political and social structures of society. Technology will be impelled in new directions to support the needed changes. As soon as the paradigm is changed, the whole path before us changes, and people awaken to a new era. But for this to occur we need another structure, another model of behavior, and a new belief system: a new value system for mindful living in a new world. There is a need for what we have named the quantum paradigm.

There are many things that need to be curated. It is essential that all people are brought into the scope of the projected Great Unity where everyone is cared for by each other according to the idea of "common good" and of the "wholeness" in the teachings of Confucius. What is required is a collective awareness and a collective approach to cherishing the environment and evolving today's societies into a bio-ecologically and bio-socially integrated functional system. Humanity must achieve this awakening and follow its journey of life and evolution.

THE RISE OF QUANTUM LEADERSHIP IN THE CHINESE PERSPECTIVE

The arrival of this new era calls for a new kind of leadership, the kind described as Quantum Leadership as we have already discussed in this book, and is further presented in the book of this title coauthored by Frederick Tsao and Chris Laszlo.[30]

This quality of leadership is essential in any process of transition. Quantum leaders must be grounded in humility, aware of the need for life learning, and conscious of the path of transformation toward holistic oneness with the universe—of flowing with the *Dao*. Consciousness is the mother of capital and the solution to all challenges. The right kind of leaders are required to lead this transformation and the people we call quantum leaders have the capacity to intuitively fulfill the purpose of humankind, which is to create and to evolve, to live authentically and naturally.

There are people in every area of life who see the impetus of the universe, listen to the *Dao,* and use it to help them to create the future. There is nothing more important in any situation, in any group, or in any society, than the quality of leadership. The rise of quantum leadership is the rise of those who promote the development of leadership fit for our current epoch—the end of the Industrial era and the dawn of the era of well-being and higher consciousness. This type of leader has the creativity to stimulate the transition.

These leaders engineer their shift in consciousness toward holism and authenticity. Humanity is part of the process of creation, and its role is to create further systems of life. To awaken to this truth is to awaken to the quantum paradigm. Quantum leaders are responsible for the process of creating further extensions to life in the context of protecting the integrity of life itself, which is holistic. To do so, they go through a four-part process—awareness, alignment, collaboration, and creation.

In the Chinese perspective, leadership for the new era is an awakening to the holism which is unity and consciousness. From this paradigm comes a new ethical system which is effectively the same as the *Dao*. All of our actions must be viewed from a holistic perspective. But to understand the wisdom of holism in our world, it is necessary to understand the nature of the systems of which it is composed, systems within systems, which is what *The Great Learning* explains. It describes the expansion of life which mimics the expansion of the universe from the self outward in a systemic and relational way.

The basic ideas of quantum leadership are incorporated in the aspirations of the current leadership in China. Today's China is to a large extent embracing these ideas by reconnecting to the culture of its past in order to address the problems it faces at present. As China develops, education is likely to play an increasingly important role in the process of its transformation. China's education system is changing course, reflecting an awareness that the upcoming new era will be one of learning with much more emphasis on traditional Chinese culture and philosophy in school curricula along with the omission of some of the modern Chinese system's more ideological elements.

China, in the not-too-distant-future, could become the world's biggest economy, and it is searching for a new paradigm compatible with globalization and today's technologically enhanced mode of life focused on sustainability. Its leaders also stress the importance of Quantum science and technology in a way that is unique among the nations of the world.

The traditional Chinese worldview includes many aspects that can be easily integrated into other worldviews. It is a system worth considering outside the context of the Chinese world because it offers a comprehensive roadmap for growth and expansion aimed at flourishing life. The world is in need of a new structural foundation for universal ethics, and the traditional Chinese system, secular and relational, is a good option to consider.

The change to a new human worldview based on the quantum paradigm will alter everything, just as several hundred years ago there was a shift to the industrial and scientific paradigm through the influence of the works of Adam Smith, Isaac Newton, Karl Marx and others. That era served its purpose and is now coming to an end. From the Chinese perspective, humanity's focus in the future will become more and more centered on learning and personal growth. As policies of education and health care change, urban living and planning will also change. As human beings grow and shift their consciousness, solutions will become more holistic. The rise of the consciousness of quantum leadership in matters of business capital will bring wisdom and efficiency to the distribution of resources to serve the era of well-being.

Human beings have a choice of how to live, and as they awaken, there is the opportunity to be part of an ideal arrangement of human society along the lines of the Chinese concept of Great Unity, a holistic, dynamic and harmonious entity, always evolving but always in sync with the endless recalibration of the universe.

Another point of reference for understanding this process is the model of Spiral Dynamics,[31] a concept to model human evolution and life published in 1974 by Claire W. Graves and refined in the works of Don Edward Beck and Christopher C. Cowan twenty-five years later. This is a color-coded eight-level system, starting with subsistence and moving through the degrees of sophistication of human society. Graves then proposed another tier beyond the current level of human evolution, to be viewed as an open spiral.[32] As Don Beck describes it in the 2002 book titled *Spiral Dynamics*,

> A spiral vortex best depicts the emergence of human systems, or memes, as they evolve through levels of increasing complexity. Each upward turn of the spiral marks the awakening of a more elaborate version on top of what already exists, with each meme a product of its time and conditions. And these memes form spirals of increasing complexity that exist within a person, a family, an organization, a culture, or a society.[33]

Regardless of what theories are applied, ancient or modern, it is clear is that humanity is advancing toward the next level of evolution in the journey of life. It is developing a higher form of consciousness with greater authenticity and alignment with oneness in the greater whole. Quantum science provides the basic concepts of the emerging paradigm, and ancient Chinese wisdom provides The Way (the *Dao* 道). The fusion of the two into one integral system is the manifestation of a new order of mindful living at the dawn of an era that promises to be the dawn of an era of well-being.

PART THREE

Paths to the New Era

CHAPTER 5

C H A P T E R   5

Approaches by Contemporary Thought Leaders

Having completed our exploration of Western science-based approaches and Eastern tradition-based paths (specifically the Chinese tradition-based path) to an era of well-being, we now present a collection of further path-breaking approaches by contemporary thought leaders.

++++

Awakening the Power of the New Human Story
by Gregg Braden

We live our lives, solve our problems, heal our bodies, and build our societies based upon the way we think of ourselves—our story.

As we embrace the discoveries showing that we live in an intelligent and connected universe rather than a sterile and empty vacuum, and that life emerged from cooperation rather than random mutations and the "survival of the strongest," the technologies that reflect these understandings become the natural solutions to the problems that seem unsolvable today.

All that stands between us and a world where clean, affordable energy is accessible to every member of our global family—where clean, healthy food is accessible to every mouth on the planet and where every human has the opportunity to live safely and strive to achieve their dreams—is *our willingness to embrace these values as our most cherished priorities.* It is this shift in thinking, the "paradigm shift" discussed in this book, that holds the power, and the promise, of the new human story: the new "quantum paradigm."

Our Story Matters

The story we tell ourselves about ourself has implications that we cannot escape. It defines the lens through which we act and react to the greatest challenges of our time. Our current responses to the changing climate, for example, as well as the global pandemic, failing economies, and the role of technology and artificial intelligence in our lives are all based in the way we we've been taught to think of ourselves. What we believe about our relationship to the earth, and ultimately to the universe itself, is the justification for the technologies that we build, the laws that we enact, and the policies that we embrace.

Our story influences how we share vital resources such as food, water, and medicine between nations. It determines why, when, and how we go to war, as well as when we choose to accept peace.

The implications of our story are woven into the fabric of everyday life. They show up as the food we choose to nourish our bodies and the way we care for ourselves, our children, and our aging parents. What we believe about ourselves even justifies our thinking for when we save a human life, and when we choose to end one. *When we think about it, our story, the popular, cutting-edge face of what in this book and previous publications by Ervin Laszlo and the Laszlo Institute is called the new paradigm—is at the core of everything we do and defines all that we value and hold dear.*

It is precisely *because* the way we think of ourselves plays such a vital role in our lives that it's important for us to get our story right. We owe it to ourselves to explain who we are, our relationship to one another and to the natural world, as honestly and truthfully as possible. This includes crossing the boundaries that have separated the sciences from one another and from the wisdom of our past. This also includes changing the existing story when that story is no longer supported by the new evidence.

While the truth of our story is important at any time, it's especially vital for us now. The reason is simple: it's because now is different. This is no ordinary time in human history. Today, the best minds of our time are telling us that we're living a time of extremes unlike anything in our past. And the choices we make in response to the extremes will lead us either to the heights of our greatest destiny, or seal the path to our darkest fate. The choice is ours to make.

Now Is Different

Our time of extremes is a unique moment in history when nature's cycles of change and human cycles of technology are converging to reveal the consequences of our thinking and worldview. It is a time when we can expect *big* shifts in the world, and big changes in our lives. And just to be clear, the shifts I'm talking about aren't necessarily bad things, or even good things for that matter. It's just that they're *big*, and they're happening now, in a way that cannot be discounted or ignored.

From the studies of respected think tanks like the Worldwatch Institute founded in 1974 to independently research critical global issues, and the World Resources Institute founded in 1982 to analyze environmental policy, to UNESCO's Millennium Ecosystem Assessment Synthesis Report, drafted by 1,300 scientists in 95 countries, it's clear that the best minds of our time have gone beyond the warnings of the past alerting us to dangerous trends of unsustainability. We're now living in the time that they forecasted in the studies, and the magnitude of the changes we're experiencing is our cue to sit up and take notice.

In 2005 *Scientific American* magazine published a special edition titled *Crossroads for Planet Earth*, which confirmed that our lifetime is no ordinary lifetime. The purpose of the issue was twofold: (1) to confirm the fact that the human race has entered a unique period in its history, and (2) to identify a number of global crises that, if left unchecked, hold the potential to end human life and civilization as we know it today.

More recently, Sir Martin Rees, professor of astrophysics at Cambridge University and a powerful voice in the scientific community, has added a new class of threats that he calls "human induced" that need to be considered as well, including cyberattacks against critical infrastructure and advances in biotechnology and artificial intelligence.[34]

The point that these organizations and others are bringing into public awareness is that each of the scenarios identified in their reports is catastrophic with implications that will impact the world for generations to come, and all are happening now. The conclusions are unanimous—we simply cannot continue living as we have in the past if we expect to survive even another 100 years on Earth. Maybe our time of extremes is best described in the words of evolutionary biologist E.O. Wilson. In the *Scientific American* essay titled "The Climax of Humanity," Wilson states that we're living a "bottleneck" in time, when the stress upon both our resources and our ability to solve the problems of our day will be pushed to their limits.[35]

It may be precisely because of the "bottleneck" that Wilson describes, and the immense implications of what such a time means in our lives, that there's been a reluctance to even acknowledge that *now* is, in fact, different. How scarce does fresh water need to become before we acknowledge that there is a problem? How many times does the world's population need to double while its resources continue to shrink? How many major banks need to fail? How close do we have to come to another global war? How bad do things have to get before we acknowledge that we're already in trouble, and already heading for even bigger trouble, unless we change the way we think?

The Good News:
We Still Have Time to Make Good Choices

There's a direct link between the way we think of ourselves and our willingness to embrace new and innovative solutions to the extremes that we face. Fortunately, the scientific community gives us a place to begin, and the reasons to acknowledge that now is no ordinary time in human history.

While the conclusion of the *Scientific American* report honestly described what we are up against as a civilization, it also offered a ray of hope, suggesting that "if decision makers can get the framework right, the future of humanity will be secured by thousands of mundane decisions."[36] It's in the details of everyday life that the "most profound advances are made."[37]

It is in this ray of hope that we discover the message of good news: We have entered a once in a civilizational opportunity to rethink the direction of our past, and to make new choices that can lead to the promise of a clean, healthy, and sustainable future for generations to come.

The Best News:
We Already Have the Solutions

While we often find ourselves focusing upon the magnitude of the extremes, and often with good reason to do so, it's easy to lose sight of the best news that comes with the extremes—

We already have the solutions to the biggest problems facing the world today! The technological solutions that is. Fortunately for us, the technology to solve the biggest challenges we face has already been discovered. The advanced principles are already understood. The biggest problems we could ever imagine are already solved. The solutions already exist in this moment, right here, right now, and are at our fingertips. The following facts are examples of what I mean.

- **Fact:** *We already have the food to feed every mouth of every child, each woman and man living on the Earth today.*

  The agriculture of the world produces 17 percent *more* calories today than it did 30 years ago, enough for at least 2,720 kilocalories per person per day.[38] The lack of food is not the reason that 690 million members of our global family are hungry today. Rather, it's the result of poverty, economic disparity, climate change, and the lack of leadership that makes feeding our global family a priority.

- **Fact:** *We already have the proven technology to create clean, reliable, electricity inexpensively from material that is abundant, produces zero greenhouse gasses, cannot be made into weapons, and cannot melt down like a nuclear reactor.*

  If we are really serious about creating large amounts of electricity reliably and consistently from an energy source that produces zero greenhouse gases, the use of thorium, element 90 on the periodic table of elements, should be at the top of our list. In addition to renewable resources such as solar, geothermal, and wind-power technology that can locally supplement conventional power sources, thorium energy is a proven technology. A number of thorium generators have already been built and have been used successfully in countries that include India, Germany, China, and the United States. In the US, there have been two Thorium generators: the Indian Point facility, which was operational between 1962 and 1980, and the Elk River facility, which was operational between 1963 and 1968.[39]

While we need more research to hone thorium technology to meet the large-scale needs of the world, it holds the promise of a stepping-stone to a clean and abundant alternative to tide us over while we engage in our search for the ultimate source of clean and abundant energy.

- **Fact:** *We already know how to reduce the abject poverty of the world that has been the source of scarcity and suffering.*

  The United Nations Millennium Development Goal to reduce the world's most extreme poverty (of those living on US $1.25 per day) is working. The first goal, to halve the proportion of the world's population who is living in such poverty between 1990 and 2015, was actually met in 2010, *five years ahead of schedule.* This tells us that real change is achievable and lays the foundation for a push toward an even greater effort.[40]

- **Fact:** *We already know how to create clean, green and sustainable economies based upon cooperation and sharing, rather than competition, lack and scarcity.*

Collaborative, or shared, economies are based upon the exchange of skills, goods, and services rather than the stockpiling of products in response to anticipated demand or shortages. Examples of businesses emerging from the principle of shared economies, include Airbnb, Uber and Lyft ridesharing, and projects made possible by crowdsourced funding. The projections for this quickly expanding, collaborative and cooperative form of commerce is projected to represent 50 percent of the traditional rental market by 2025.

• Fact: *We already know how to create sustainable and self-sufficient communities that rely upon localized sources of food, economy, energy, education, and healing.*

From the Damanhur federation of 600(+) residents living in communal, educational, and spiritual community in Northern Italy, to the self-sufficient rammed-earth homes of the Earthship communities in Northern New Mexico, and Arizona's Arcosanti community founded by renowned architect Paolo Soleri, the decades-long success of localized living has been proven in alternative communities throughout the 20th, and now into the 21st century. In times of extremes, these communities are less vulnerable, and more resilient, to disruptions in vital supply chains, disease from centralized and contaminated produce, breakdowns in large economies and loss of electricity from centralized power grids.

• Fact: *We already have the proven knowledge to reverse common disease, reverse aging and trigger the healing of every organ and gland in the human body.*

The recent discoveries of a new class of neurons in the human brain, new class of stem cells that remain vital regardless of age, and the 40,000 sensory neurites in the human heart add to the growing body of evidence that we are wired to heal and thrive through the ability to self-regulate our biology.

When we consider these facts, it's clear that the solutions to our biggest challenges of energy, climate, economies, and healing have already been discovered. The advanced principles are already understood. The technology already exists. The obvious question is simply *"Where are these solutions today?"* The answer to this question is perhaps the best news of all, because it doesn't hinge upon circumstances that are beyond our control. It also highlights what may be the greatest crisis that we face as a global family—a crisis in thinking.

Our thinking is the very key to the way we deal with the needs of the emerging world. You and I are being tasked with something that has never been done. We are being challenged to radically shift the way in which we think of ourselves and our relationship to the world—*to change our story, shift our paradigm*—and to do so faster than any generation in history has ever done before. As we learn to make our most cherished values such as life, health, community, and creativity the number one priority in our lives, the existing solutions become our natural response, rather than the exception, to our world of extremes.

The choice to accept what the discoveries have revealed, and to implement the technologies that can ease so much suffering in our world, rests solely upon our answer to a single question:

Are we willing to embrace the new discoveries—the new paradigm and human story—that makes such possibilities a priority in our lives? To embrace a new human story, it makes sense to recognize the existing story that we have been led to believe in the past. As discussed in chapter two of this book, for over 300 years, students of the modern world have been steeped in a scientific theory that tells us (1) we are the product of purely random processes and biological luck that seems to defy all odds, and (2) that we exist in a dead universe that is the result of equally random processes and extraordinarily lucky cosmology.

If it were true that we live in a dead universe made of inert stuff, like the dust of exploded stars or debris from colliding asteroids and disintegrated planets, then it would actually make sense to do what we've done in the past, which is to exploit every resource available, to the highest degree possible, and reap the benefits and rewards of those resources. New discoveries, however, show that both of these beliefs are obsolete. And because they are no longer the story of life and the universe, they can no longer be our story, as well.

Beyond Lucky Cosmology

There is an emerging scientific thinking that sees the universe as a living and conscious entity. At the forefront of this new paradigm and what it means in our lives are the publications of the Laszlo Institute of New Paradigm Research, and of researcher and educator Duane Elgin. Elgin's philosophy, the same as the work of Ervin Laszlo himself, is based upon existing evidence in the scientific community that the universe is like a living entity that is growing and evolving rather than a passive lifeless system.

Both Elgin and Laszlo show us that the way we think of the universe and of our place in it is at the very foundation of the way we live our lives and solve our problems, even on a daily basis. This is especially true when it comes to how we treat one another.

From the new story/new paradigm perspective, it is no coincidence that our habits of consumerism and the exploitation of natural resources reflects the worldview of a lifeless cosmos. It is this belief that's led us to think of the world as a vast repository of resources that's ours to dominate. In Elgin's words, we relate to our belief that we're in a lifeless universe "by taking advantage of that which is dead on behalf of the living. Consumerism and exploitation are natural."[41] With rare exceptions, this is how societies in the past have been conditioned to think and to live. The problem with this mind-set is that, ultimately, it has led to the depletion of limited resources, unsustainable forms of food production, and the conflicts that are at the root of so much suffering today.

New-paradigm research has revealed that we are part of a living system, and that knowing our true relationship to the cosmos can change how we relate to one another on a daily basis and in the end will lead us toward a more sustainable world of cooperation. The parallels that exist between what we observe in living systems and what we've observed throughout the universe lend credence to this view. From microbes and neural networks, to ecosystems and the behavior of entire populations, all living systems, regardless of their size, show characteristics that demonstrate the sharing of both energy and information. In support of this theory, Elgin describes qualities of the known universe that reveal:

- That it is completely unified and able to communicate with itself instantaneously in nonlocal ways that transcend the limits of the speed of light [42]

- That it is sustained by the flow-through of an unimaginably vast amount of energy [43]

- And that it is free at its deepest, quantum level [44]

While these traits, in and of themselves, don't necessarily confirm that we are part of a living universe, their existence adds to a growing body of information that suggests that we are. By extrapolation, as living beings we cannot separate ourselves from this cosmic exchange of energy and information. The discoveries identified in Elgin's work and in the work of Ervin Laszlo and the Laszlo Institute give us good reasons to rethink the universe itself, and our place in it. If the universe is more than lucky cosmology at its best, then it makes sense that there's more to us than lucky biology, primal competition, and survival of the strongest. The best science of the modern world agrees.

Beyond Lucky Biology

New discoveries ranging from human evolution and genetics to the emerging science of neuro-cardiology (the bridge between the brain and the heart) have overturned 150 years of scientific thinking when it comes to the way we think of ourselves in the world. The new human story tells us that we showed up on Earth approximately 200,000 years ago as what scientists today have named *Anatomically Modern Humans* (abbreviated as AMH). While the scientific community is largely in agreement with this date of our appearance, it's the way that we arrived that's the source of controversy.

The nature of our existence is in direct violation of the evolutionary principle put forth by Alfred Wallace, Darwin's co-discoverer of evolution theory. The principle states "nature never over-endows a species beyond the needs of everyday existence." In other words, features that give us an advantage for survival appear only as the need for them arises throughout our existence. The problem is that we arrived with a host of extraordinary capabilities already in place and the potential for others to be developed, in a way that far exceeded the needs of everyday existence. In other words, from the perspective of biology, we are overendowed on a level of many magnitudes.

For example, when we appeared 200,000 years ago *we already had* a brain 50 percent larger than our nearest primate relatives. And within our brain, *we already had* neurons that are unique to humans, including the "rosehip" neuron that regulates targeted information flow in our neocortex. *We already had* the mysterious fusion that created our chromosome 2 and gave us our uniquely human capacity for empathy, sympathy, compassion, and the self-regulation of our biology On-Demand. We already had the 40,000 sensory neurites in our heart creating a unique neural network that thinks, feels, learns, and remembers independently of the cranial brain. *We already had* the uniquely human capacity to create coherence between our heart and our brain, and the ability to do so On-Demand—to optimize our biology, physiology and cognitive potential. And *we already had* much more.

The key here is that these features did not develop slowly, gradually, over a long period of time in response to a biological need as evolution theory suggests. We've had these features from day one. When we compare our DNA today to the DNA extracted from the remains of Anatomically Modern Humans of the past, we discover that we haven't changed physically. We have the same brain size, the same cranial capacity, the same body proportions, the same DNA, and the same extraordinary potential that our ancestors had thousands of years ago.

And while the science has yet to fully solve the mystery of our emergence, it tells us clearly that while evolution is a fact recorded in the fossil record for many forms of life, something beyond evolution as we know it has contributed to our existence, and our extraordinary potential.

The New Paradigm: The New Human Story

Over 150 years ago, geologist Charles Darwin published his paradigm-altering book titled *On the Origin of Species by Means of Natural Selection*. His book was intended to provide a scientific explanation for the diversity of life in general, and the origin of modern humans specifically. In one of the great ironies of the modern world, since Darwin's time, the very science that was expected to strengthen and support his theory has done just the opposite. The most recent discoveries are revealing facts that fly in the face of long-standing scientific tradition. Among these facts are the following.

- **Fact 1:** The fundamental principle of nature is based upon cooperation and mutual aid, and not the competition, struggle and "survival of the strongest" that Darwin proposed in his 1859 theory.

- **Fact 2:** The relationships shown on the conventional human tree of evolution are not based on physical evidence. While these links are believed to exist by some scientists, they've never been proven and are *inferred* or *speculative* relationships.

These facts, and a host of others which are based upon peer-reviewed science, clearly do not support the conventional narrative of the past that we've been taught. It is for these reasons that we need a new paradigm, a new story to accommodate the new evidence. Or conversely, we need to follow the evidence we already have to the new and unifying story that it tells.

We're Not What We've Been Told, and More Than We've Believed

In the past, we have all been led to think of ourselves in ways that have that helped us make sense of our world—through stories based on what our families and communities accepted as true at some given point in time. If we're honest with ourselves and acknowledge the fact that the world is changing, then it makes sense that our stories must change as well. Our ability to successfully meet and transcend the challenges that are converging in our lives begins with the most obvious, yet difficult, question we could ask of ourselves: *How can we navigate our time of extremes if we're not honest about the discoveries that tell us who we are?* Our willingness to acknowledge the magnitude of this simple question is the key to our success in our time of extremes.

As a society, we now find ourselves at a meeting point of two ways of thinking about our relationship to the world around us. The new paradigm and Elgin's living universe offer us the big picture of life having a purpose from the top down—from the macro scale of the universe as a living entity, within which, at the micro scale, the living cells of our bodies express themselves. The new discoveries of precise mutations revealed from the fossilized DNA offer the evidence from the bottom up—from the micro world of mutated chromosomes yielding more complex expressions of life within the big picture of the living universe. From this systems-thinking perspective, the new discoveries and the story they tell, change everything.

In the emerging paradigm of the universe, our physical existence is sustained by an aliveness that is inseparable from the larger universe. Seeing ourselves as part of the unbroken fabric of creation awakens our sense of connection with, and compassion for, the connection, the oneness and the totality of life. In Elgin's words, "We recognize our bodies as precious, bio-degradable vehicles for acquiring ever-deepening experiences of aliveness."[45] The new paradigm tells us that we are part of the world, and not separate from it. It reminds us that our aliveness is part of an even greater aliveness. And because the very goal of life is to grow, evolve, and perpetuate itself, these are precisely the qualities that it makes sense for us to embrace the laws, policies, and technologies through the course of our lives.

Through each experience we face in life—through the satisfactions and the frustrations of every job, through the ecstasy and the heartbreak of each intimate relationship, through the unspeakable joy of bringing a child into this world, or the unbearable pain of losing a child, through the choice to take another human life and the ability to save a life, through each war that we create and every time we end a war—in all of these experiences and so many more, we learn to know ourselves better as individuals, as communities, and as a species. Each time we push ourselves to the edge of what we believe, we discover that there's more to know. We get to experience our aliveness through new eyes and relish it, if we choose to do so. And to do so is the very definition of a living universe, and our role in it. Albert Einstein's work in science and philosophy led him to precisely this conclusion.

As is the case with so many scientists who strive to unlock the deepest mysteries of our existence, the deeper their discoveries take them, the more they recognize that there's something more to human existence than a random and meaningless universe would produce by accident. When Einstein was asked about the nature of existence, his response was elegant. Following is an excerpt of Einstein's thoughts in order to give context to the answer that I have emphasized in italics.

A human being is a part of the whole, called by us "Universe," a part limited in time and space. He experiences himself, his thoughts and feelings as something separate from the rest—a kind of optical delusion of his consciousness. This delusion is a kind of prison for us, restricting us to our personal desires and to affection for a few persons nearest to us. *Our task must be to free ourselves from this prison by widening our circle of compassion to embrace all living creatures and the whole of nature in its beauty.* Nobody is able to achieve this completely, but the striving for such achievement is in itself a part of the liberation and a foundation for inner security.[46]

The beauty of Einstein's statement is that it transcends physics, numbers, and logic. It is a purely intuitive answer to a serious scientific question. It is also a perfect example of how advances in modern science have carried us to the edge of what science can tell us with certainty. There is a place—an unspoken boundary—where the nuts and bolts of scientific explanation fail when it comes to describing us and our story. They do so because we're more than cells, blood, and bones that can be measured. There's a quality to human life—to us—that simply cannot be defined in purely scientific terms, at least as we know science today. And it's that quality that can lead us to comprehend the deepest truths of our existence.

To discover that we exist as living beings within the context of an even larger living system implies that our lives are about something more than simply being born, enjoying a few years on earth, and dying. It implies that somewhere, underlying everything we know and see, our lives have purpose. Science fiction writer Ray Bradbury may have said it best: "We are the miracle of force and matter making itself over into imagination and will. Incredible. The life force experimenting with forms. You for one. Me for another. The universe has shouted itself alive. We are one of the shouts." [47]

We may discover that the existence of our extraordinary and advanced capabilities such as intuition, sympathy, empathy, and compassion hold the key to unlocking the mystery of the new human story. No other form of life on Earth has the capacity to love selflessly, to embrace change by choice in a healthy way, to self-heal, to self-regulate longevity, or to activate the immune response on demand. And no other form of life has the capacity to experience deep intuition, sympathy, empathy, and ultimately, compassion—all of which are expressions of love—and to do so on demand. These uniquely human experiences are telling us that our lives have purpose, and the purpose may be as simple as embracing these abilities to know ourselves in their presence.

The Question

Without a doubt, each of us will be faced with life-changing decisions in the near future. Perhaps the most profound, as well as the simplest, of those decisions will be to embrace what the new discoveries have shown us about who we are and about our relationship with the cosmos, one another, and perhaps most importantly, with ourselves. If we can accept, rather than deny, the powerful evidence that reveals the new human story, then everything changes. With that change we can begin anew. In the presence of our own deep truths, the technologies that align with our relationship to nature and the living essence of the cosmos become the measure of our evolution.

Ultimately the question that we must each ask ourselves is an even simpler one: Do we love ourselves enough to live in our lives, what we know in our heart is possible? The choices that we make in each moment of our lives is our answer, as well as the legacy that we leave for our children and the generations to follow.

++++

Human Well-Being and the Pathless Path
by Deepak Chopra

As soon as you begin to think about human well-being, one mystery piles on top of the other—Why are so many people unhappy? Why do we do things guaranteed to cause pain and suffering? Is there a secret key to well-being that needs to be discovered the way Einstein discovered relativity? Yet the most baffling mystery is also the most basic: Are humans even designed to be happy?

Evolution serves as a kind of Providence for other creatures, giving them food, shelter, and mating privileges. These are the gifts that come with survival. A lion devouring a gazelle doesn't consider its victim's suffering or feel guilty of murder. But humans are different. Evolution released us from its grip, and for at least 30,000 years, every newborn among Homo sapiens arrives in the world with the same higher brain that modern humans possess. This implies that well-being is deeply changed—when you can think about your own existence, nothing is predestined. You can create your own well-being.

This open-ended existence leads to what J. Krishnamurti called the first and last freedom. In other words, it is where every life begins and ends. There is nothing beyond freedom; once you have it, you have it. But the greatest gift has a dark side. For countless people an open-ended existence is intolerable. A writer faced with writer's block looks upon a blank sheet of paper with despair. Infinite combinations of words and thoughts are possible, and yet having infinite choices is paralyzing.

Even when an open-ended existence isn't intolerable, it creates problems. Having too many choices takes most people very far out of their comfort zone. (Marketers say that the secret of McDonald's worldwide success is that it offers the possibility of choice on its menu, but basically only one food, the hamburger, is on the menu.) To solve the burden of too many choices, every society has operated using what Aldous Huxley called a "reducing valve." The infinite variety of possibilities is squeezed down to a manageable few.

Sometimes the reducing valve leads to benign results. Models were established that promised abundant fulfillment if a person adhered to the things that are proven to promote well-being. The Japanese have a concept known as *Ikigai*, which is defined as "a reason for being." If you can attain Ikigai, whose roots can be traced back to traditional Japanese medicine, your life will be fulfilled. To get there, a person must take action aimed at four main goals:

Love

Things you are good at

An affordable lifestyle

What the world needs

There's a moral basis to this model: Existence has no value if these four areas are not fulfilled. You can't count up love the way you can count up brands of peanut butter, frozen pizzas, and cars, yet we all know the difference between emptiness and fullness in matters of love. *Ikigai* opens our eyes to how a life of purpose and meaning is constructed. The concept, which is part of daily life to millions of Japanese, originated on the island of Okinawa at an unspecified date in the past, although the word *Ikigai* itself can be traced to as early as the 8th century A.D.

One virtue of *Ikigai* that doesn't appeal to Western society is that it puts everyone on the same page, keeping the common good foremost in mind. Individuality is secondary. This is considered important by a people as conformist as the Japanese. But there is no novelty in ascribing well-being to the purpose-driven life, or to rooting your purpose in something you passionately believe in—both concepts are centuries old.

Ultimately, conformity is stifling. Another ancient model focuses on the individual and is therefore less restrictive. This is the fourfold model found in India, where to this day children are taught that the four aims of life, as laid down in the Vedic spiritual tradition, are *Artha, Kama, Dharma,* and *Moksha.*

Artha is prosperity in material terms.

Kama is fulfillment of love, pleasure, and desires in general.

Dharma is morality, finding a righteous way to live.

Moksha is spiritual fulfillment through liberation or inner freedom.

The words in Sanskrit shouldn't mislead us into thinking that these are merely Indian concepts. The reason that a child born in any generation, including me, was taught these four values is that they have universal appeal. By implication all four goals are attainable by anyone. Moreover, life will become distorted unless one pays attention to each goal. Look around and you will witness the imbalance that results when only *Artha,* or material prosperity, and *Kama,* the pursuit of desire, dominate to the exclusion of the moral and spiritual side of life. Morality and spirituality add meaning to human existence, and the one thing human beings cannot tolerate for long isn't poverty but a meaningless life.

If we cut to the quick, all models for achieving well-being are fatally flawed by using the reducing valve. When infinite possibilities are squeezed down into a few possibilities, advocated for our own good, the price is too high. Instinctively, children rebel when a parent says, "It's for your own good," and the same is true when we are faced with formulas for well-being. Traditional cultures have their good points, no doubt, but this doesn't explain why the Japanese, Chinese, and Indians flee in vast numbers away from their traditions into the arms of Westernized living.

At the risk of massive generalization, the Western approach to well-being is based on a root concept: progress. One generation expects to have more well-being than the previous generation because external conditions keep improving. No one doubts that modern medicine has eliminated a huge swath of disease that created centuries of misery. The Industrial Revolution—or several Industrial Revolutions—created modern advanced Western societies with all the conveniences we take for granted.

But progress is merely a concept, and to believe in it you must overlook everything that contradicts the concept. Looking around, the contradictions are many, and for countless people the result is misery. Witness the ever-climbing rates of anxiety and depression, maladies that remain incurable since tranquilizers and antidepressants only palliate the symptoms rather than addressing the cause. Science has improved our lives, but at the diabolical cost of atomic, biological, and chemical weapons, which hang like a cloud of terror over the world.

You might agree with the most optimistic futurists like Yuval Harari in his book *Homo Deus*, where he declares on the first page that war, poverty, and plague have finally been solved, and still the result isn't guaranteed to increase human happiness. In advanced Western economics, when asked if they are thriving or merely surviving, only 30 percent of people say they are thriving—this is in countries that have free health care, free education, and adequate retirement benefits.

I could expand this survey *ad infinitum*, but enough has been said to reinforce the mystery that is at the heart of the matter: Are humans even designed to be well? Forget violence, crime, and domestic abuse. Set aside so-called lifestyle disorders like heart disease, diabetes, and hypertension, which skew sharply upward in rich countries. Even put on the back burner the mounting levels of stress that many experts judge to be the root cause of lifestyle disorders, depression, and anxiety.

These are all sidetracks. The question of human well-being, as I see it, comes down to our open-ended existence. Freed from the grip of Darwinian evolution, gifted with Krishnamurti's first and last freedom, has human nature imploded on itself? Unlike the lion who suffers no qualms killing and devouring a graceful, beautiful, innocent gazelle, we are either cursed or blessed with self-awareness. So which is it?

You can't google the answer or look it up on Wikipedia. You can't turn to traditional models, and in modern secular society, you probably wouldn't look to organized religion. The only answer that works is the one that works *for you.* Well-being and all of its synonyms—wellness, fulfillment, holistic health—is a do-it-yourself project. I think everyone instinctively realizes this fact, and embraces it. The Western belief in progress is flawed, but it has the great advantage of opening life to experimentation.

In this case, scientific experimentation doesn't work. Since I was trained as a medical doctor, I am not pushing science aside as a matter of ignorance or prejudice. But the whole point of a scientific experiment is to arrive at consensus. In 1628 William Harvey discovered that the heart pumped blood in circular fashion throughout the body. This phenomenon was provable through conducting various experiments, and quickly there was universal consensus.

But the same isn't true for human well-being. Nothing you can measure, count, and collect data around will define, much less predict, what will make you happy, right now or forever. This objection hasn't discouraged mountains of research into human psychology. Principally the focus has been on mental disorders, and the definitive handbook in psychiatry, the DSM-5 (Diagnostic and Statistical Manual of Mental Disorders), currently lists 300 mental illnesses. That's an achievement in diagnosis; the achievement in cures is marginal, unfortunately. Only recently did a new field spring up, known as positive psychology, whose aim was to increase well-being rather than cure mental disorders.

You'd suppose, thanks to its upbeat name, that positive psychology might make significant advances in making people happier. But the findings are mixed at best. First, it was discovered that people are bad at predicting what will make them happy. The traditional answers—getting married, having a baby, developing a successful career—don't work for everyone, and all have an undertow of increased stress. Having more money works up to certain point, basically the point at which your finances are secure. Beyond that, adding more money doesn't bring more well-being.

The second, more controversial finding, is that lifelong or constant well-being is a myth. The best we should hope for is a state of inner contentment that falls very short of bliss, ecstasy, and joy.

The third finding is that each person does have freedom of choice over creating his or her own well-being. I cannot vouch for how this figure was arrived at, but we're told that around 40 percent of a person's well-being or happiness depends on personal choice, the remaining 60 percent being laid down to genetics, family history, social conditioning, and external forces like racism, poverty, and disease.

What I extract from this muddle is roughly this: Well-being is a do-it-yourself project because it has to be. Unless you are willing to sacrifice your freedom and squeeze your life through the reducing valve, you must go on a personal journey, and this journey points inward. In the tradition of Yoga, there is no map to guide you on this journey. It is a pathless path (which brings up another lovely adage from Krishnamurti, "Truth is a pathless land.")

If someone desired to begin the inner journey today, or wanted to recommit to a journey that has been frustrating so far, I will risk offering some advice. The purpose of the inner journey is transformation. No one has been cursed with freedom, but there are wise ways to use it and not so wise ways. The not-so-wise ways have been fully explored in modern society, and it's time to discard them. Endless consumerism, online distractions, a glut of entertainment, and all the trappings of a rich Western society have nothing to offer.

Therefore, if we truly want to be transformed, I think some practical resets work very well.

Reset 1: Stay centered

In everyone's life, stress is unpredictable and takes control when it gets to be too much. Then we are thrown off balance mentally and emotionally. The people who respond the best to chronic stress know how to remain centered. They can consciously return to a state of calm inner balance. This is a skill you can apply right now and every day in the future.

Anytime you feel agitated, distracted, restless, scattered, or on the verge of being overwhelmed, take a few minutes to center yourself. Find a quiet place, close your eyes, take a few deep breaths, and place your attention on the middle of your chest in the area of your heart. Sit quietly, breathing normally, until you feel calm and centered. The key to this practice is repetition. By doing this often during the day, meaning anytime you notice that you are not centered, you accustom your mind to returning naturally and easily to its balance point.

Reset 2: Find and give support

People survive crises better if they have as much support as possible. Studies have shown that each support system you add to your life increases your sense of safety, security, and well-being when times get tough. Support can come from family, friends, religious affiliation, service organization, and various support groups online and in the community.

Finding support for yourself and giving it to others is a basic form of bonding, and it counters the impulse to be alone and isolated, which is very common in a crisis. Support is the opposite of constantly texting, seeking distractions, and being online all day. The time to create a web of support around you is during good times, so that when things are not so good, you have a psychological and emotional safety net.

Reset 3: Value inner peace and quiet

Slowdowns, lockdowns, and enforced isolation are boring. There's a feeling of passivity and uselessness that sets in for many people. So the urge to get moving once more is only natural as the crisis wanes. But you need to realize that the mind can fall easily into boredom and restlessness because it is in the habit of being in constant activity. Modern life puts our nervous systems into overdrive, and most people are addicted to this, mistaking overstimulation for normality.

The best remedy for nervous-system overdrive is to take time every day to go inside and wind down. Learn to value your mind's inner quiet and calmness. This is a state of awareness that is at once restful and alert. In-time isn't dead time. You are becoming comfortable with the set point from which all creativity and productivity springs.

Reset 4: Raise your spiritual I.Q.

Everyone is living a unique story, even when society experiences a mass event like the pandemic. An essential part of anyone's story needs to be a set of higher values. These include love, compassion, empathy, beauty, truth, creativity, service, devotion, and personal growth. Unless you actively spend time engaged with these values, in whatever way you choose, you are not using your spiritual potential.

By devoting yourself to the higher values you have chosen, you raise your spiritual I.Q. You can't be spiritual just by wishing or dreaming about it; even regular meditation, although valuable, isn't the same thing. You have to express your spirit, which only happens in everyday life. Purpose and meaning grow if you nourish them, and the best way to do this is by consciously leading a life in which spiritual values are given real priority.

Reset 5: Cultivate detachment

It is hard to define detachment and even harder to put it in a positive light. In modern life the emphasis is always on doing, improving, getting involved, making a career, and so forth. In other words, there is constant pressure to be fully engaged all the time. Yet there's a reason behind biblical teachings like God's message in Psalm 46:10 to "Be still, and know that I am God" and "Be in the world but not of it." The Buddhist doctrine of "non-doing" points in the same direction but without religious overtones.

The point of detachment, which is the common thread in all these teachings, is that it leads to a great mystery. This is the mystery of higher consciousness, also referred to as waking up, becoming enlightened, and walking in the light. To grasp what "waking up" means, you can't rely on your ego and isolated self. They are mental constructs that keep you totally entangled in the world and its cycles of pleasure and pain.

When you cultivate detachment, you can go inside and experience a state of awareness untouched by the ups and downs of existence. You shift your identity away from the insecure, isolated ego-personality. Instead you rely on something society never teaches us, that consciousness and existence are united. In this union life becomes simple yet perfected, because despite all our endless activity, being fully conscious achieves bliss, freedom from fear, and access to the field of infinite possibilities.

There are all kinds of experiences that aid in this transformation: freeing yourself from the judgment of others, discovering that you are lovable, and feeling safe and secure in yourself, knowing that you are valued in the cosmic plan. But these resets aim to be a basic guide. They are based on the personal answer I arrived at when confronted with the most fundamental mystery" Are humans even designed to be well? I say yes, but there's no point quoting chapter and verse from the world's wisdom traditions, which support my yes. Well-being, as happiness, remains a do-it-yourself project. It helps to have a vision of where the journey is leading you. Beyond that, the adventure begins.

++++

The Time-Reverse Approach:
Lessons from the Year 2050

by Hazel Henderson

Dateline 2050

As we move into the second half of our twenty-first century, we can finally make sense, from an evolutionary system perspective, of the origin and impact of the coronavirus that struck the world back in 2020. Today, in 2050, looking back on the past forty turbulent years on our home planet, it seems obvious that Earth had taken charge of teaching our human family. Our planet taught us the primacy of understanding of our situation in terms of whole systems, identified by some far-sighted thinkers, scientists, and visionaries as far back as the mid-nineteenth century. This widening human awareness revealed how the planet actually functions, its living biosphere systemically powered by the daily flow of photons from our mother star, the Sun.

Eventually, this expanded awareness overcame the cognitive limitations and incorrect assumptions and ideologies that had created the crises of the twentieth century. False theories of human development and progress, measured myopically by prices and money-based metrics such as GDP, culminated in rising social and environmental losses: pollution of air, water, and land; destruction of biological diversity; loss of ecosystem services, all exacerbated by global heating, rising sea levels; and massive climate disruptions.

These myopic policies had driven social breakdowns, inequality, poverty, mental and physical illness, addiction, loss of trust in institutions—including government, media, academia, and science itself—as well as loss of community solidarity. They had also led to the pandemics of the 21st century, SARS, MERS, AIDS, Ebola, influenza, and the various other coronaviruses that emerged back in 2020.

During the last decades of the 20th century, humanity had exceeded the earth's carrying capacity as the Global Footprint and Nine Planetary Boundaries research had shown. The human family had grown to 7.6 billion by 2020. Western-style industrialization and globalization had continued its obsession with economic, corporate, and technological growth that had caused the rising existential crises threating humanity's very survival. By driving this excessive growth with fossil fuels, humans had heated the atmosphere to such an extent that the United Nations (UN) climate science consortium IPCC noted in its 2020 update that humanity had only ten years left to turn this crisis situation around. The winter of 2019–2020 in the Northern Hemisphere was the warmest since records had begun.

As far back as 2000, all the means were already at hand: we had the know-how and had designed efficient renewable technologies and circular economic systems based on nature's ecological principles. This was clearly tracked in such reports as the Green Transition Scoreboard, which documented the global shift away from fossil fuels and nuclear power, now historically recorded in "Mapping the Global Green Transition, 2019–2020." By 2000, patriarchal societies were losing control over their female populations because of the forces of urbanization and education. Women themselves had begun to take control of their bodies, and fertility rates began to tumble even before the turn of the twenty-first century. The politicizing of surgical abortion was ended after women simply circulated the abortion and contraception pills worldwide by mail. Widespread revolts against the top-down narrow economic model of globalization and its male-dominated elites led to disruptions of the global supply chains and other unsustainable paths of development driven by fossil fuels, nuclear power, militarism, profit, greed, and egocentric leadership.

Military budgets that had starved health and education needs for human development gradually shifted from tanks and battleships to less expensive, less violent information warfare. By the early 21st century, international competition for power focused more on social propaganda, persuasion technologies, infiltration, and control of the global internet. In 2020, the coronavirus pandemic's priorities in medical facilities competed with victims in emergency rooms, whether those were wounded by gun violence or patients with other life threatening conditions. In 2019, the nationwide US movement of schoolchildren had joined with the medical profession in challenging gun violence as a public health crisis. Strict gun laws gradually followed, along with rejection of gun manufacturers in pension funds' assets crippling the gun lobby, and in many countries, guns were purchased back by governments from gun owners and destroyed, as Australia had done in the 20th century. This greatly reduced global arms sales, together with international laws requiring expensive annual licenses and insurance, while global taxation reduced the wasteful arms races of previous centuries.

Conflicts between nations are now largely governed by international treaties and transparency. Now in 2050, conflicts rarely involve military means, shifting to internet propaganda, spying, and cyber warfare. Early social media companies driven by advertising profits had led to unanticipated consequences of fueling terrorism along with racism, hate, and xenophobia, distorting childhood development. Irresponsible behaviors were actually encouraged by their marketing algorithms designed by psychologists' persuasion technologies to be addictive and engender outrage. These led to huge profits due to network effects and the free use of the internet platforms developed by taxpayers and government research. These unanticipated social consequences led to the revival in 2022 of the social innovation of technology assessments and other futurist scenario research methods. By 1974 in the USA, these technology assessments were mandated to anticipate the likely social and environmental impacts of all technological innovations on those groups most vulnerable, whether for profit or as policy. This first governmental Office of Technology Assessment (OTA) produced far-reaching anticipatory reports (still today available in digital form from the University of Florida Press). This OTA model was followed by others in forty countries, but in the USA it had been shuttered in 1996 by a Republican Congress.

By 2020, these disruptions of global business as usual exhibited all the fault lines in human societies: from racism and ignorance, conspiracy theories, xenophobia, and scapegoating of "the other," to various cognitive biases—technological determinism, theory-induced blindness, and the fatal widespread misunderstanding that confused money with actual wealth.

Money, as we all know today, was a useful invention: All currencies are simply social protocols (physical or virtual tokens of trust), operating on social platforms with network effects, their prices fluctuating to the extent that their various users trust and use them. Yet countries and elites all over the world became enthralled with money and with gambling in the "global financial casino." This further encouraged the seven deadly sins over traditional values of cooperation, sharing, mutual aid, and the Golden Rule.

Scientists and environmental activists had warned for decades, in hundreds of technology assessments and similar reports, of the dire consequences of these unsustainable societies and retrogressive value systems, but until the 2020 pandemic, corporate and political leaders and other elites stubbornly resisted these warnings. Previously unable to break their intoxication with financial profits and political power, it was their own citizens who forced the re-focus on the well-being and survival of humanity and the community of life. Incumbent fossilized industries fought to retain their tax breaks and subsidies in all countries as gas and oil prices collapsed. But they were less able to buy political favors and support of their privileges. It took the global reactions of millions of young people, "grassroots globalists," and indigenous peoples, who understood the systemic processes of our planet Earth—a self-organizing, self-regulating biosphere which for billions of years had managed the planetary evolution without interference from cognitively-challenged humans. The Nature's Principles taught as "biomimicry" by ecologically-focused groups stressed how such principles had allowed life to evolve successfully on planet Earth for over 3.8 thousand millennia.

In the first years of our twenty-first century, the earth responded in an unexpected way, as it had so often during the long history of evolution. Humans' clear-cutting large areas of tropical rainforests and massive intrusions into other ecosystems around the world had fragmented these self-regulating ecosystems and fractured the web of life. One of the many consequences of these destructive actions was that some viruses, which had lived in symbiosis with certain animal species, jumped from those species to others and to humans where they were highly toxic or deadly. People in many countries and regions, marginalized by the narrow profit-oriented economic globalization, assuaged their hunger by seeking "bush meat" in these newly exposed wild areas, killing monkeys, civets, pangolins, rodents, and bats for additional protein sources. These wild species carrying a variety of viruses were also sold live in "wet markets," further exposing ever more urban populations to these new viruses.

Warnings by ecologists of the need to protect and restore forests and biota and to refrain from factory farming of animals for food were summarized as far back as the 1960s and 1970s in the best sellers *Silent Spring* (1962), *The Closing Circle* (1971), and the Club of Rome report *"Limits to Growth"* (1972) as well as the books *Diet for a Small Planet* (1971) and *Small Is Beautiful* (1973). Back in the 1960s, for example, an obscure virus jumped from a rare species of monkeys killed as bush meat and eaten by humans in West Africa. From there it spread to the United States where it was identified as the HIV virus and caused the AIDS epidemic. Over four decades, this caused the deaths of an estimated 39 million people worldwide, about half a percent of the world population. Four decades later, the impact of the coronavirus was swift and dramatic. In 2020, the virus jumped from a species of bats to humans in China, and from there it rapidly spread around the world, decimating world population by an estimated 50 million in just one decade.

From the vantage point of our year 2050, we can look back at the sequence of viruses SARS and MERS, and the global impact of the various coronavirus mutations that began back in 2020. Eventually such pandemics were stabilized, partly by the outright bans on "wet markets" all over China in 2020. Such bans spread to other countries and global markets, cutting the trading of wild animals and reducing vectors, along with better public health systems, preventive care, and the development of effective vaccines and drugs. Yet killing animals for meat diets continued because of the vested interests of the incumbent corporations. This continued until animal rights vegan and vegetarian movements and investor groups financed the rapid expansion of today's plant-based foods and beverages sectors, as well as cell-grown meats and insect-based foods. Pollinating insects are now protected and considered vital to fertilizing our foods, while growing trees and plants for fuel is banned, restricted only to algae grown on saltwater, one of our basic resources for many uses.

The lessons for humans in our tragic 50 years of self-inflicted global crises—the afflictions of pandemics, flooded cities, burned forestlands, droughts, and other increasingly violent climate disasters—were simple. Many were based on the discoveries of Charles Darwin and other biologists in the nineteenth and twentieth centuries:

- We humans are one species with very little variation in our basic DNA.

- We evolved with other species in the planet's biosphere by natural selection, responding to changes and stresses in our various habitats and environments.

- We are a global species, having migrated out of the African continent to all other continents, competing with other species and causing various extinctions.

- Our planetary colonization and success in this Anthropocene Age of our twenty-first century, was largely due to our abilities to bond, cooperate, share, and evolve in ever larger populations and organizations.

- Humanity grew from roving bands of nomads to living in settled agricultural villages, towns, and mega-cities of the twentieth century where over 50 percent of our populations lived. Until the climate crises and those of the pandemics in the first years of our 21st century, all forecasts predicted that these mega-cities would keep growing and that human populations would reach 10 billion by today, in 2050.

Now we know why human populations topped out at the 7.6 billion in 2030, as expected in the most hopeful scenario of the IPCC as well as in the global urban surveys by social scientists documenting the decline of fertility in *Empty Planet* (2019). This scenario turned out to be driven not only by the fertility crash engendered by women, the effects of urbanization and education, but also as a result of the de-globalization that occurred after the 2020 pandemic and re-localization of food production and many human activities. The newly aware "grassroots globalists" often referred to their agendas as "glocalization." The armies of school children, global environmentalists, and empowered women joined with green, more ethical investors and entrepreneurs in localizing markets. Millions were served by microgrid cooperatives powered by renewable electricity, adding to the world's cooperative enterprises, which even by 2012 employed more people worldwide than all the for-profit companies combined. They no longer used the false money metrics of GDP. In 2015 they switched to steering their societies according to the UN's Sustainable Development Goals (SDGs), the 17 goals of sustainability and restoration of all ecosystems and human health.

These new social goals and metrics all focused on cooperation, sharing, and knowledge-richer forms of human development, using renewable resources and maximizing efficiency. This long-term sustainability, which is equitably distributed, benefits all members of the human family within the tolerance of other species in our living biosphere. Competition and creativity flourish with good ideas driving out less useful ones. This is enhanced by science-based ethical standards and deepening information in self-reliant and more connected societies at all levels from local to global. These necessary reforms were often led by the 16 Principles of the Earth Charter, ratified worldwide by all sectors at all levels in most countries, which was launched in the Peace Palace in The Hague in 2000. The Earth Charter continues today; it is based in Costa Rica, the first country to end its military, and still guides us as a complementary balance to the Universal Declaration of Human Rights in 1947.

When the coronavirus pandemic struck in 2020, the human responses were at first chaotic and insufficient but soon became increasingly coherent and even dramatically different. Individualism and competitive approaches were balanced by collective action and community responsibility, including the work by millions of volunteers. Global trade shrunk to only transporting rare goods and shifted to trading information. Instead of shipping cakes, cookies, and biscuits around the planet, we shipped their recipes and all the other recipes for creating plant-based foods and beverages. Locally we installed green technologies: solar, wind, geothermal energy sources, LED lighting, electric vehicles, boats, and even aircraft. Politicians in many industrial "overshoot" countries backed the fundamental shift to these kinds of technologies in their massive "green infra-structure" plans they once derided.

Fossil fuel reserves stayed safely in the ground, as carbon was seen as a resource, much too precious to burn. The excess CO_2 in the atmosphere from burning fossil fuel was captured by organic soil bacteria, deep-rooted plants, billions of newly planted trees, and in the widespread rebalancing of the human food systems based on agrochemical industrial agribusiness with advertising and global trading of a few monocultured crops. The over-de-pendence on fossil fuels, pesticides, fertilizers, and antibiotics in animal-raised meat diets that was based on the planet's dwin-dling freshwater had proved to be unsustainable. Today, in 2050, our global foods are produced locally from saltwater agriculture and include many more overlooked indigenous and wild crops and all the other salt-loving (halophyte) food plants whose com-plete proteins are healthier for human diets.

Mass tourism, and travel in general, decreased radically, along with air traffic and phased-out fossil fuel use. Commu-nities around the world stabilized in small- to medium-sized population centers that became largely self-reliant with local and regional production of food and energy. Fossil-fuel use vir-tually disappeared. By 2020 it could no longer compete with rapidly developing renewable energy resources and correspond-ing new technologies and upcycling of all formerly-wasted resources into our circular economies of today. Because of the danger of infections in mass gatherings, the sweat shops, large chain stores, as well as sports events and entertainment in large arenas gradually disappeared. Democratic politics gradually became more rational since demagogues could no longer assemble thousands in large rallies to hear them. Their empty promises no longer hog our precious internet and were also curbed in social media, as these profit-making monopolies were broken up by 2025 and now in 2050 are regulated as public utilities serving the public good in all countries.

Education has expanded worldwide, often a freely available service online, while all on-site public education is focused on the UN's 17 SDG goals and fully-funded so that tuition and student loans are things of the past. Examples of sustainable, systems-based education are the renowned Schumacher College in Britain and the Capra Course, taught by physicist and systems theorist Fritjof Capra, author of *The Tao of Physics* (1982) and other bestsellers.

Network-based servant leaders are no longer blocked by the curse of money in politics that was finally outlawed by publicly-financed elections. All the mass gatherings were reduced as mailing in paper ballots gradually became legal in most democratic countries, along with mandatory voting in many. We all learned that we now live in "mediocracies" whatever our ostensible forms of government. Voters keep a wary eye on ambitious TV and movie celebrities who try to run for public office.

The global-casino financial markets collapsed along with their magical thinking—the pyramiding of fictional "derivatives" all based on stoking greed or fear to push stocks in financial media. In reality, all economic activities were driven not by "efficient markets" in textbooks but by the psychological processes of herd behavior. Markets, which have always evolved from barter and trading early shells, cows, and wampum, shifted back from the financial sector to credit unions and public banks in our cooperative sectors of today. The manufacture of goods and our service-based economies revived traditional barter and informal voluntary sectors with local currencies as well as numerous non-monetary transactions that had developed during the height of the pandemics. As a consequence of wide-spread decentralization and the growth of self-reliant communities, our economies of today in 2050 have become regenerative rather than extractive, and the poverty gaps and inequality of the money-obsessed, exploitive models have largely disappeared.

Crypto currencies based on blockchains and algorithms succumbed as speculation gave way to reality by 2025. There were sad experiences of losses, fraud, "forking" of presumably permanent rules, rigidity of smart contracts, and the eroding of promised trust. Trust, as we now know, is based in face-to-face community and personal relationships and proved too hard to scale! The question always became, "who owns the blockchain?" and "how is this crypto tethered to a real world asset?" The answers were a blow to the speculators and those who placed their faith in computer algorithms, the so-called "cloud" and the idiocy of connecting everything to the over-burdened internet, which crashed from the overuse during the successive waves of epidemics.

These further tribulations and the related cuts and blackouts in fossil electricity overloaded grids in 2020 and 2021 spurred the rapid shift to our renewably-powered, circular economies of today. The pandemic of 2020, which crashed global markets, finally upended the ideologies of money and market fundamentalism. Central banks' tools no longer worked, so "helicopter money" and direct cash payments to needy families, such as pioneered by Brazil, became the only means of maintaining purchasing power to smooth orderly economic transitions to sustainable societies. This shifted US and European politicians to prioritizing their creating of new money (in the past relegated to central banks) and these government stimulus policies replaced "austerity." They were rapidly invested in renewable resource infrastructure in their respective Green New Deal plans.

When the coronavirus spread to domestic animals, cattle, and other ruminants like sheep and goats, some of these animals became carriers of the disease without themselves showing any symptoms. Consequently, the slaughter and consumption of animals dropped dramatically around the world. Pasturing and factory-raising of animals had added almost 15 percent of annual global greenhouse gases. Big meat producing multinational corporations became shorted by savvy investors as the next group of "stranded assets" that included fossil fuel companies Some switched entirely to plant-based foods with numerous meat, fish, and cheese analogs. Beef became very expensive and rare, and cows were usually owned by families, as in earlier times, on small farms that produced local milk, cheese, and meat, along with eggs from their chickens.

After the pandemics subsided, and populations in many countries acquired "herd immunity" when expensive vaccines were developed, global travel was allowed only with the immunity or vaccination certificates of today, used mainly by traders and wealthy people. A majority of the world's populations now prefer the pleasures of community and online meetings and communicating, and the precious resources of the internet were rationed by guidelines to assure essential public services and health facilities have priority. Traveling is cherished, particularly locally by public transport, electric cars, and by the solar and wind powered boats we enjoy today. As a consequence, air pollution has decreased dramatically in major cities around the world. With the growth of self-reliant communities, so-called "urban villages" have sprung up in many cities—redesigned neighborhoods that display high-density structures combined with ample common green spaces. These areas boast significant energy savings and a healthy, safe, and community-oriented environment with drastically reduced levels of pollution.

Today's eco-cities include food grown in high rise buildings with solar rooftops, vegetable gardens, and electric public transport after automobiles were largely banned from urban streets in 2030. The streets were reclaimed by pedestrians, cyclists, and people on scooters browsing in smaller local stores and craft and farmer's markets. Solar electric vehicles for inter-town use often charge and discharge their batteries at night to balance electricity in single-family houses. Free-standing solar-powered vehicle recharger units are available in all areas, reducing use of fossil-based electricity from obsolete centralized utilities, many of which were bankrupt by 2025.

After all the dramatic changes we enjoy today, we realize our lives are now less stressful, healthier, and more satisfying, and our communities can plan for the long-term future. To assure the sustainability of our new way of life, we realize that restoring ecosystems around the world is crucial so that viruses dangerous to humans are confined again to animal species where they do no harm. To restore ecosystems worldwide, our global shift to organic, regenerative agriculture flourished, along with plant-based foods, beverages, and all the saltwater-grown foods and kelp dishes we enjoy. The billions of trees we planted around the world after 2020 at the time of our agricultural improvements gradually restored our ecosystems.

As a consequence of these changes, the global climate has finally stabilized, with today's CO_2 concentrations in the atmosphere returning to the safe level of 350 parts per million. Higher sea levels will remain for a century, and many cities flourish on safer, higher ground. Climate catastrophes are now rare, while many weather events continue to disrupt our lives, just as they had in previous centuries. The multiple global crises and pandemics, caused by our earlier ignorance of planetary processes and feedback loops, had widespread tragic consequences for individuals and communities. Yet we humans have learned from our many painful lessons. Today, looking back from 2050, we realize that the earth is our wisest teacher, and its terrible lessons may have saved humanity and large parts of our shared planetary community of life from extinction.

++++

The Spiritual/Mythical Approach to the Era of Well-Being

by Jean Houston

The discovery of the quantum nature of our universe is so major an event that it can literally transform the course of human history. Its profound revelations and implications cannot be overstated. The great 800-pound Gorilla in the room can no longer be avoided. And that is Consciousness! Quantum theory demands a radical re-visioning of the role of consciousness as the underlying organizing principle of the universe. With this understanding, quantum physics is introducing us to ways of seeing which profoundly impact human thinking, feeling, sensing, knowing and being, myth and archetype. The deeper knowledge of this, the kind taken not only into the mind, but into the heart, viscera, spirit, and soul, changes us profoundly. It can radically affect us and move us into speciation, that is, to the emerging evolutionary development of humankind, to the portals of a new era of well-being that bring us to our inherent possibilities for experiencing our quantum identity and quantum consciousness.

We are living in the uprising of the myth. We are becoming in fact "mything" links! How many of you are experiencing the nature of this new reality—the rising of the depth currents of all times, all cultures and all experiences? Its effects are felt not just in the fascination with myth, the seeking of spiritual experience, the revival of the knowings of indigenous people, the coming of a world music that incorporates and sustains the knowings of many regions, the wildly interesting styles of clothing that mix and match continents on a single body, the food! Even on the shadow side, we find rising for a last stand the old tribal gods in their varying fundamentalist postures: tricksters playing with power, archaic fascist forms, and populist rising of the dictatorial narcissists before they are swept—not away, nothing is ever swept away—but into a new amalgam in which they, too, become part of the larger story. Today, and for all of us, all parts of the planet are catching all parts of the planet including the past, the future, and the cosmic!

In order to prepare for the new era, the human psyche is manifesting many different singularities of itself as it helps the planetary movement toward convergence and transition. Our psyche is moving at remarkable speeds past the limits most of us have lived with for thousands of years into an utterly different state of being. The contents of the psyche are manifesting at faster and faster rates in a dreamlike reality in which it is difficult to tell any more what is news and what is drama, what is matter and what is myth. We live in chaos which we may have created in order to hasten our own meeting with ourselves. All over the world, in virtually every culture I visit (I worked in 109 countries), I find that images that were relegated to the unconscious are becoming conscious. Happenings that belonged to extraordinary experiences of reality are becoming more common, and many of the maps of the psyche and its unfolding are undergoing awesome change.

Some years ago I found myself sitting on the ground in a small village in India watching a television dramatization of the Ramayana. The village's one television set was a source of great pride, and all the villagers had come in from their fields and houses to be inspired and entertained by the weekly hour in which the many episodes of this key myth of the Hindu world were so gloriously produced. The story told of Prince Rama (an avatar of the God Vishnu) and his noble wife, Princess Sita (a human incarnation of the goddess Lakshmi), and how they had been betrayed and banished to live in a forest for fourteen years. Nevertheless they are very happy, for Rama is noble, handsome and full of valor, while Sita is virtuous, beautiful, and completely subservient to her husband. They are, in other words, the archaic ideal of the perfect married couple. Unfortunately, their forest idyll is brutally interrupted when Sita is abducted by the many headed, multi-armed demon, Ravanna, who promptly carries her off to his own kingdom of Sri Lanka. Enter the saintly monkey Hanuman, who with his army of monkeys and bears, along with Rama, is eventually able to vanquish Ravanna and his formidable troops of demons and rescue Sita. Rama takes her back, however, only after he is convinced of her virtue and the fact that she not once "sat on the demon's lap."

There is never a minute in the Hindu world when this story is not enacted, sung, and performed in a puppet show or a

Balinese shadow play, or in a stage or screen performance. It is the core myth of the Hindu psyche. And this television series was a lavish treatment filled with spectacular effects, exotic costumes, thrilling music and dance, and acting appropriate to the playing of the gods. The villagers were as entranced as I, for this was religion, morality, and hopping good musical theater all in one. Furthermore, they were joined together in the knowledge that all over India, at that moment, hundreds of millions of people were watching this program with the same fascination. Suddenly, the old Brahmin lady who owned the television set and who was sitting next to me on the ground turned to me and said in lilting English, "Oh, I don't like Sita!"

"Pardon?" I was aghast. This was like my Sicilian grandmother saying that she doesn't like the Madonna.

"No, I really don't like Sita. She is too weak, too passive. We women in India are much stronger than that. She should have something to do with her own rescue, not just sit there moaning and hoping that Rama will come. We need to change the story."

"But the story is at least three thousand years old!" I protested.

"Even more reason why we need to change it. Make Sita stronger. Let her make her own decisions. You know, my name is Sita and my husband's name is Rama. Very common names in India. He is a lazy bum. If any demon got him, I would have to go and make the rescue."

She turned and translated what she had just said to the others who were sitting around. They all laughed and agreed, especially the women. Then the villagers began to discuss what an alternative story, one that had Sita taking a much larger part, might look like. It was a revisionist's dream, listening to people whose lives had not changed much over thousands of years actively rethinking their primal story. It was like sitting in a small town in southern Mississippi listening to Christian fundamentalists rewrite the Bible. Astonished and exhilarated, I sensed that I was experiencing in this village a beginning stage of the re-invention of myth, the advent of a new era. No matter that this primal tale was ancient beyond ancient, and venerable beyond venerable; it belonged to an outmoded perception of women and their relationship to men and society, and it had to change or go.

I should tell you that back in that village in India when the beautiful episode from the Ramayana ended, and following the commercial interlude, the next program that all of India was watching was the prime-time soap opera of some seasons ago, *Dynasty*! As I watched the dubious comings and goings of the characters, I didn't know where to hide my head. My hostess saw my embarrassment at the comparative low level of American television and patting my arm said, "Oh, sister, do not be embarrassed. Don't you see? It is the same story."

"How can you say that?"

"Oh, yes, indeed," she continued, her head wagging from side to side. "It is the same story. You've got the good man. You've got the bad man. You've got the good woman. You've got the bad woman. You've got the beautiful house, the beautiful clothes, the people flying through the air. You've got the good fighting against the evil. Oh, yes, indeed, it is the same story!" Thus are myths and metaphors recast, so redesigning the human fabric and all our ways of seeing.

It is our privilege and our particular challenge to witness and assist a new era coming into being. As actors in this new era, we are seeing the evolution of old archetypes, and the rise of new archetypes. Look at just one of them—seamlessness.

To begin, one of the great powers is simply the fact of seamlessness, sometimes called the ground of being, sometimes called the quantum vacuum, sometimes called the Akashic field. And we arise out of this seamlessness. The universe is one. It's there when we talk about the invisible universe which comes as dark matter out of which everything arises. We are 99.9 percent pure generativity; 99.9 percent of you is the realm that gave birth to the universe. You are a mode of the universe, a mode of Earth, a mode of the cosmos, the latest unfolding experience, a creation of the metabolism of the galaxy, and this seamlessness is probably what David Bohm referred to as the implicate order that harbors everything. It is that 99.9 percent which is the realm of being itself, and out of which everything is generated. What is this seamlessness? It rises up and refines itself through definition. And as you think, as you dream, as you define, as you engage, then what happens is this cosmic foam collapses—this probability wave collapses until it results in something. The art and science of creativity and manifestation has to do with your ability to bring pattern and form into this great foam, this great, pure, creative energy which is the wave of seamlessness. You create a new wave. This is how you co-create an era of well-being with the universe. In terms of the hero's journey, it is the great call to the larger life; it is the invitation to your larger destiny. Out of this energy of pure potential, your pattern, your ideas, your intention, your desire calls from this seamlessness, this wave of a new probability.

Patterns of millennia have prepared us for another world, another time, another era. At the same time, the virus pandemic, unlike any ever known in human history or pre-history, has confused our values, uprooted our traditions, and left us in a labyrinth of misdirection. Factors unique in human experience are all around us-—the inevitable unfolding towards a planetary civilization, the rise of women to full partnership with men, the daily revolutions in technology, the media becoming the matrix of culture, and the revolution in the understanding of human and social capacities. The Zeit is getting Geisty as the old story itself is undergoing the sacred wound in order that it too grows and addresses the multiples of experience and complexity of life unknown to our great grandparents. We have become so full of holes that perhaps we are well on the way to becoming holy. Thus I now must address the issues of wounding.

Soul-making begins with the wounding of the psyche by the larger story. Soul-making requires that you die to one story to be reborn to a larger one. So too is your wounding, the breaching of your soul, an invitation to your renaissance. Our woundings tell us that old forms are ready to die, however reluctant the local self is to allow this to occur. And that hitherto unsuspected new forms are ready to flower. As the ties that bind loosen in our culture and in our psyche, the incidence of woundings accelerates and comes in many disguises. (*Some pretty weird*).

Wounding often involves a painful excursion into pathos, wherein we experience massive anguish and the suffering cracks the boundaries of what we thought we could stand. And yet, time and again, I discover that the wounding pathos of our own local story contains the seeds of healing and even of transformation. This is an often-told truth and is woven into all classic tales of the human condition. Witness the Greek tragedies in which the gods force themselves symptomatically into consciousness at the time of wounding. All myth, in fact, has wounding at its core. I continually joke that Christ must have his crucifixion; otherwise, there's no upsy-daisy. Artemis must kill Acteon when he comes too close. Job must have his boils. Dionysius must be childish and attract Titanic enemies who rip him apart. An abundance of sacred wounding marks the core of all great Western myths and their attending gods and humans: Adam's rib, Achilles' heel, Odin's eye, Orpheus's decapitation, Inanna's descent and torture, Prometheus's liver, Zeus's split head, Pentheus's dismemberment, Jacob's broken hip, Isaiah's seared lips, Persephone's rape, Eros's burnt shoulder, Oedipus's blinding, and so it goes on and on, wounding after wounding.

We are drawn to these stories over and over. We do not flinch before their terrors, although they may mirror our own.

Is this because they carry us into the mystery, the marvel, the uncanny, the announcement that with wounding, the sacred enters into time? Each prefigures a journey, a renaissance, a turning point in the lives of gods and mortals. From the point of the wounding, the journey of gods and humans proceeds towards new birth, and with it, the unfolding of a sensuous acuity to the needs of others that was not possible before. Being more vulnerable, we reach out, we extend our hands and our hearts to others who are wounded. It is only at such a pass that we grow into a larger sense of what life is about and act, there-fore, out of a deeper and nobler nature.

There is no question but that wounding opens the doors of our sensibility to larger reality, which is blocked to our habitu-ated and conditioned point of view. Pathos gives us eyes and ears to see and hear and feel what our normal eyes and ears and feel-ings cannot. Thus I offer the conundrum that as baby-making occurs through the wounding of the ovum by the sperm and the sperm's explosion and dying into the ovum, so soul-making occurs through the wounding of the psyche—quite possibly by the gods. And by "gods" I mean not old atavisms, but those psychospiritual potencies yearning at the threshold of existence to enter into time and through our lives to "redeem the unread vision of the higher dream." Maybe the gods also suffer and even die, as we do, out of their old archaic selves, to be rebirthed as emergent culture, art, story, spirit, or science.

Having taken depth-probings of the psyche of many people the world over, I feel this to be so. I know that in the West we have moved from the Promethean myth of snatching fire from heaven to the myth of Proteus, the shape-shifter. The sea-god Proteus was capable of taking on all manner of shapes, forms, and purposes at will. This is us today confronting the dawn of a new era. Suddenly, like Proteus, we have to become protean— highly resilient and creative, able to adapt to the ever changing story—especially in the light of constant challenge, and ever present peril. As Robert J. Lifton who has written wonderfully of the relevance of the Proteus archetype for our time has said, "Without quite realizing it, we have been evolving a sense of self appropriate to the restlessness and flux of our time." Something is calling.

When we undertake to consciously work with the great old myths, a rich and varied world of experience opens to us. We can travel with Odysseus, experience the passion play of Isis and Osiris, wander with Percival in search of the Grail, and die and be reborn with Jesus. Within the spoken or ritually enacted myth we can allow our lives to be writ larger, the personal particulars of our local existence finding their amplification and elucidation in the personal universals of the greater story and the larger characters which myth contains. Those of us who work with myth, like many of the Jungians, David Feinstein, and ourselves, find that our clients and students, having entered the realm of the ancient stories and their persona, seem to inherit a cache of experience that illumines and fortifies their own. They soon discover that they too are valuable characters in the drama of the world soul, pushing the boundaries of their own local story and gaining the courage to be and do so much more.

How then can we change patterns so deeply woven into the structure of our psyches? Up until recent decades, I doubt that one could have done much more than alter certain details. Now, however, in a time of crisis, when everything is deconstructing and reconstructing, myth too requires its redemption. It is as critical a task as one could attempt in this new millennium—how to actually go about changing the dominant myths by guiding people into the realms of the psyche wherein they have the power to change their own essential story. We work on the premise that all over the world psyche is now emerging, larger than it was. We are experiencing the harvest of all the world's cultures, belief systems, ways of knowing, seeing, doing, being. What had been contained in the "unconscious" over hundreds and thousands of years is up and about and preparing to go to work. What had been part of the collective as the shared myth or archetype is now finding new rivers of unique stories flowing from out of the passion play of individual lives.

With so much more history, with so much more experience behind us and within us, we have achieved what is surely an extraordinary evolutionary achievement: the ability to continually receive, recreate, reframe, and extend our experience. This new protean capacity of the self is virtually a new structure of mind, brain, and psyche—for it grants us the capacity to view ideas and systems, be they social, intellectual, political, or philosophical and spiritual—with a freedom that was not ours in the past.

In my Mother/Father's house are many mansions. Maybe so, but part of our job is to help provide the furniture and set up housekeeping in the rooms of these mansions that heretofore were relatively uninhabited by our conscious minds. As we begin to enter the geography of the inscapes, we discover many ways and means of entering and enjoying the uniquely personal worlds and wonders that lie within. We are gathering an ensemble of methods to travel and train in inner space. These include guided imagery, dream incubation, working with the Inner archetypes, in a kind of time travel in the mind-brain system. One is taken on journeys back and forward in time, so that you may heal old wounds and transform obstacles into opportunities. New powers will be opened as you learn to reframe your story as a myth, finding within your own body the metaphors for conflict and conciliation, discovering powerful personal shields and inner allies. Always reconnected to the luminous myths of generations past, you are led to become a pioneer in the undiscovered continent of the myths of an era now dawning.

Since culture is everywhere being newly reimagined, nothing is more necessary than a rebirth of the self. These are times that are meant to breach our souls, unlock the treasures of our minds, and, through the divine act of mythologizing, release the purpose, the plan, and the possibilities of our lives. We are re-grown to greatness and take our place with Percival and Penelope, with White Buffalo Woman and the Lady of the Lake, with Quetzalcoatl and Bridget and Dr. Spock.

* * *

A good deal of my work has had to do with helping create an era that offers well-being to all. The era of well-being embraces the understanding of the world as an ecology, a complex adaptive system in which global and universal awareness is applied to local concerns. It is based on a new order of relationships in which male and female, science and spirituality, economics and ecology, civic participation and personal growth, story and myth, and the self and the quantum field come together in an integral and interdependent matrix for the benefit of all.

We humans are not alone as we face the massive transition that is upon us. Rather, we are embedded in a larger ecology of being, its motive force arising simultaneously from the planet that is our birth place and the stars that are our destination. Pulsed by Earth and Universe toward a new stage of growth, we are waking up to the realization that we can become partners in creation—stewards of the Earth's well-being and conscious participants in the cosmic epic of evolution. As ancient peoples have always known, the story is bigger than all of us, and yet desires our engagement, our love, and our commitment. We are part of the cosmological unconscious. The powers of the Universe are studying themselves through us—what an opportunity.

Teilhard said that the natural depth of each one of us is the whole of creation. And the truth of this is so real and astonishing that it's often not understood. As Thomas Berry said, "We are articulating stardust. How can we not drop to our knees breathless in wonder and overwhelmed with gratitude?"

Teilhard saw this. He says that we are the generation that is awakening to the stupendous fact that we are the universe reflecting on itself and thus emerging, evolving into new and more complex forms. A different order of archetypes . . . an Exo-type . . .

Over many years, I have studied the metaphysical cosmologies of ancient Hindu and Buddhist epistemology and spirituality and the practices of the indigenous shamanic forms of these and found, given their different metaphors, that they are remarkably similar to findings at the frontiers of quantum physics. One discovers that in both ancient texts as well as shamanic practice, consciousness is central to the nature of reality.

A study of Eastern and Western philosophies and indigenous worldviews provides practices that can deliver us not only from our chronic woes, but also bring us to our higher purpose as a member of a universe in evolution. Then, too, this emerging understanding of reality based on the quantum paradigm and the accumulation of evidence regarding the active role of consciousness in the world and cosmos not only brings about a world shift in our perspective but gives us the basis for a whole new story. This story is at once very ancient and ever new. It gives us perspective on the nature of reality and the nature of consciousness that could well affect much of our human agenda in science, mythology, theology, philosophy, psychology, and the entire spectrum of our human condition. It could even provide the basis for a Renaissance of self and society, a revolution in human possibilities beyond technological enhancements.

The quantum universe has an outer body and an inner mind. The infrastructure of one's mind mirrors these deeper quantum structures of the universe. In different states of consciousness we can be brought to subtle levels of the mind that expand to certain states of interacting with the Universe itself in what the Buddhists call "interdependent co-arising." These include states such as meditation, trance-like contemplation, rapture, ecstasy, loving, heightened creativity, and other varieties of altered states of consciousness. In these, one gains access to dynamic levels of mind that have an unbounded field of awareness of the universal field of consciousness. The self within its own unbounded nature is in some sense identical to quantum mind and therefore has many more capacities than those operating in local consciousness. The deepest values, the deepest purpose, the deepest patterns for life, the richest potential codings for existence are then available. Within the level of creative patterns, not unlike the Platonic forms, one finds that great ideas and innovative actions become manifest. We have seen that these meditators, mystics, and highly creative persons more readily see these cosmic connections, these potential entry points into the cosmos, and they "return" full of potential and creative ideas in way beyond where they would ordinarily exist in their given point in space and time. They are known to have focused on an intent that sets up reverberations which then form the objects of their intention because they are working with the quantum field to perceive revelations from a higher source or cosmic consciousness.

The extraordinary part is that when we are able to bring local consciousness to a higher resonance in the quantum field, we access news in and from the universe. In this state, the all-knowing is direct knowing in real time, and all systems are go. In these states, we are engaging a beyond-spacetime realm that is consonant with our deep mind or creative unconscious from which everything arises. This is ultimately a spiritual experience and a cosmic connection. It is a quantum connection. And it is all part of the great hologram of existence, every part entangled with every other and working together.

Quantum physics points out that it makes no sense whatsoever to talk about the universe as if it exists objectively, separate from us, or to talk about us existing independently of the seemingly outer universe. The universe and we are inseparable partners in a timeless embrace. We are collaboratively dreaming up the universe, while the universe is simultaneously dreaming us up according to the Buddhist concept of "interdependent co-arising." What a game!

But within this game lies the paradox of being human. Here we are, we local beings living in a biodegradable spacetime suit that allows us to persist for a number of years doing our local Earth-based objectives. But we are also mythic nonlocal infinite beings with quantum powers and possibilities that give us the chance to live in a universe larger than our aspirations and more fascinating than our dreams. And in this time of such great challenge, when because of virus pandemics and the avalanche of avarice and ignorance, the human experiment could come to an end within a few decades, the wonder is that principles and knowledge have arisen from cosmology and the great discoveries and experience of the intrepid explorers of the nature of consciousness, the spiritual reality that is the ground of our existence. So together, beginning in the late 19th and early 20th Century, there has been the coming of two phenomenal happenings almost simultaneously: the harvest of the wisdom of the world's spiritual traditions, and the revolution in physics that brought us the quantum nature of reality. My old friend and coauthor Deepak Chopra has wonderfully expressed what results from these two happenings when he said, "The future of God is the evolution of our own consciousness from separation to unity, from a fragmented mind to a whole mind, from thought which is in time to Awareness which is not in time."

Spacetime and matter not only originate in the Akashic field, the primordial quantum ground of infinite energy and quantum flux but also are constantly sustained by it. The physicist David Bohm suggests that below the quantum field "there are even more subtle levels of process that are involved in loops of active information. This whole hierarchy extends to increasingly more subtle levels in which both matter and consciousness are contained." In a sense therefore, the universe may have emerged in a "big bang" or as thought lately, a big bounce out of a limitless energy. "But looked at in another light, even this is only a small ripple within the immense activity of the ground, which in its turn arises out of an eternally creative source that lies beyond the orders of time."

At this deep subtle level, therefore, there is no direction to time, neither past nor present nor future, but there is evidently a simultaneity to time—time past, time present, and time future occurring all together concurrently in ways that are difficult for us to understand, given our conditioning to think in terms of the "arrow of time," habituated as we are to present and future following relentlessly from the past with no side trips allowed.

Thus in the quantum world, all events can exist concurrently, and to all practical purposes everything is correlating with everything else. The universe is entirely alive and interconnected through the medium of this quantum reality—for as present scientific speculations suggests, information transmits through the bridges or wormholes connecting all points with all others in an indefinite number of possible patterns, constantly changing and turning on and off at incredible frequencies of up to 10 to the 43rd power of times per second. Either that, or we exist in a quantum hologram projected from beyond spacetime, and within which we are all entangled and resonant with each other. We are amphibious beings with regard to time and space, living in a cosmic hologram our several lives of self and psyche at the same time.

And if you add to this the conundrum of certain aspects of quantum physics that suggests all possible futures are here right now, and that we stand at a cross roads in which we can select from one as the other futures go on in parallel universes—then you have a much more complex reality of unconsciousness with regard to time. For this would imply that in our so-called unconscious mind lies not only the repressed or forgotten experiences of our life, but dig a little deeper and you have the experiences of ourselves in different dimensions of time and space.

Consider Jennifer, who in one reality has Lyme disease. Jennifer in another reality does not have the disease, so she visits this alternate reality or time and consults with the healthy version of herself. She reports that she even had an experience of being in the healthy, disease-free body of her alternate self in the parallel world. When she returns, she has been impacted by the experience and immediately feels healthier. Without the symptoms and fatigue she is inspired to find the kind of medical help that helps her cure any remaining aspects of the disease.

We can easily dismiss this kind of phenomenon as strong suggestion in an altered state of consciousness that then affects health and well-being. However, after having seen dozens of these kinds of learnings, changes, and shifts with several dozen students, you cannot close your accounts with reality and come to surmise that something much more interesting is happening. If there is any truth to this matter it is no wonder that we want to keep the lid on this multi-temporal unconscious! And yet perhaps these different worlds or times of our experience are not self-contained but bleed through in other states of consciousness—dreams, reveries, creative inspirations, and spiritual and other potent experiences. Including déjà vu. Consider Hildegard. . . .

The poets seem to know the same thing but express it with different kinds of words. T.S. Eliot writes in *Burnt Norton*:

Time present and time past
Are both perhaps present in time future
And time future contained in time past.

And Walt Whitman writes in *Leaves of Grass* on crossing the eons of time and being with you the reader:

Full of life now, compact, visible,
I, forty years old the eighty-third year of the States,
To one a century hence or any number of centuries
    hence,
To you yet unborn these, seeking you.
When you read these I that was visible am become
    invisible,
Now it is you, compact, visible, realizing my poems,
    seeking me,
Fancying how happy you were if I could be with you
    and become your comrade;
Be it as if I were with you. (Be not too certain but I am
    now with you.)

How do we bring ourself into this expanded experience and use of time? Our understanding drawn from the assertion of quantum physics of the simultaneity of times past, present, and future can be used in altered states of consciousness to "change" a minor happening in a person's past so that it affects their present and future in positive new ways. One is, in a sense editing the Akashic field. We can remember and even recreate the past and the future. Memories can be changed on this simultaneous all-at-once continuum in which the universe, including all its times, experiences and dimensions can be changed, transformed, rewritten, re-experienced because the universe which includes our time and memory is regenerating itself every nanosecond. Since we are conscious participants in the living universe, we can enter the Akashic fields of memory and shift elements of our own history.

Consciousness is the basic reality of the cosmos. *Your* consciousness is a precious shoot, a green tendril of this enormous beyond-spacetime One-Consciousness.

Poet Christopher Fry wrote the following in his verse drama *A Sleep of Prisoners,*

> Thank God, our time is now, when wrong
> Comes up to meet us everywhere,
> Never to leave us till we take
> The greatest stride of soul man ever took.

This stride of soul must carry us through every shadow towards an open possibility, in a time when everything is quite literally up for grabs. We can do no less. The psyche requires its greatness, as do the times.

"A new phylum still looking for our roll." The role of the human, I believe, is to provide a vessel for an era of genuine well-being, a greater order of potentials and possibilities to come forth into the universe.

++++

Healing Our Selves, Healing Our Planet
by Bruce Lipton

"You have to know the past to *understand* the present."

—CARL SAGAN

First, the Bad News: If you follow the world's news, browse the web, or if you have even looked out the window, you may have noticed *something* is going on. In the face of social, political, and economic upheaval, religious violence, racial bloodshed, climate change and a devastating global healthcare crisis, civilization is in a state of massive upheaval.

Individually, these global crises represent the "trees" in a forest we are now experiencing as the Earth's 6th Mass Extinction Event. Five times in the history of this planet, the web of life was thriving and then some cataclysmic event wiped out up to 90 percent of all plant and animal species. Each of these waves of extinction were precipitated by natural events, such as the movement of tectonic plates, massive volcanic eruptions, extensive earthquake activity and periods of radical climate change. The last mass extinction event occurred 66 million years ago when a large comet crashed into the Yucatan peninsula. This collision upended the environment, wiping out most of planet's flora and fauna and ending the reign of dinosaurs.

Today, statistics reveal that we are now deep into Earth's 6th Mass Extinction Event. According to Living Planet Report

2020, globally monitored population sizes of mammals, fish, birds, reptiles, and amphibians have declined an average of 68 percent between 1970 and 2016.[48] Scientists have recognized that as a consequence of ocean pollution, over-fishing, and destruction of fish breeding grounds, there will be no fish left in the planet's oceans by 2048. Following 27 years of surveying insect populations in Germany's national parks, the latest data reveal that insect biomass has declined by greater than 75 percent over this time period.

A study sponsored by NASA's Goddard Space Flight Center has determined that global industrial civilization is facing an *irreversible* collapse due to unsustainable resource exploitation and an increasingly unequal wealth distribution.[49] (ref: 2014).

The fate of civilization is further compromised by the impact of climate change. Rising sea levels are an immediate threat to the massive populations living on the continental coastlines. An even more devastating and less recognized impact of climate change is that the unpredictability of weather will precipitate a global catastrophe in food production.

While the previous five mass extinctions were caused by natural events, science has recognized that the current 6th extinction is due to human behavior undermining the planet's ecosystem.[50] Despite twelve years of warnings from scientists, there have been little or no government or public efforts to forestall this impending catastrophe.

Finally . . . the Good News: Since the activities of civilization have precipitated the current wave of extinction, it must also be recognized that a change in human behavior could reverse our self-imposed environmental destruction. The *good news* is that from the ashes of our failing civilization, the seeds for a new, sustainable civilization are currently germinating.

However, between the *bad news* and the *good news*, by necessity, there is a period of *chaos*. Since our current way of life is responsible for our life-threatening predicament, the only way to survive is to dismantle conventional behavior in order to build a better world on a new, sustainable foundation. Unfortunately, the media continuously focus on the scary news of the breakdown of our civilization and ignore the fact that there is also an emerging new order of life, a new civilization that is evolving.

To illustrate that point, consider the metamorphosis of a caterpillar evolving into a butterfly. Monarch caterpillars are a voracious organism that have a heavy footprint on their environment. After Monarch caterpillars hatch from eggs laid on their favorite food plant, milkweed, within a few days they will have stripped the plant of all of its leaves. The caterpillar's body is comprised of a community of millions of cells. Each of its sentient cells, the equivalent of miniature humans, is employed in carrying out the caterpillar's life functions. Some are muscle cells responsible for the organism's movements, other cells are involved with harvesting and digesting food, while still others provide for respiration and excretion, among other systemic functions.

When caterpillars run out of food, they encase themselves in a cocoon within which life-sustaining functions cease. The caterpillar's cellular community breaks down, forming a soup of "unemployed" cells. Specialized imaginal cells within the soup offer the community a new vision for a more advanced version of their civilization . . . the creation of a butterfly, an organism that has a light touch on the environment. The cocoon's cellular community experiences chaos as the caterpillar structure is breaking down, while simultaneously, the structure of the butterfly is being assembled.

In this analogy, human civilization, expressing the voracious appetite of a caterpillar, has been destroying its environment. As civilization's organization is falling apart, the human equivalent of imaginal cells is offering the public opportunities to create a more sustainable version of civilization, one with a smaller footprint on the environment. Citizens experiencing the current planetary chaos have two choices: either hold on for dear life to the failing system, or, let go and participate in the evolution of a more sustainable humanity.

The symptoms civilization is now experiencing are a message from Mother Gaia: We must either change our voracious behavior or perish in extinction. Civilization as we have known it is coming to an end. However, there is a very important fact we must recognize; this not the first-time civilization has faced its demise. Civilizations are living systems and as such, they express a life cycle comprised of a birth, a period of maturation, followed by a period of dysfunction, decline, and ending.

The Western world has already experienced the rise and fall of several civilizations. Previous cycles of civilization evolved from *animism* (e.g., the planet's Indigenous People), to *polytheism* (e.g., Romans, Greeks, Egyptians), to *monotheism* (e.g.,

Judeo-Christianity), and to our current version of civilization, *scientific materialism.*

Past, Present and a Vision for the Future: To thrive into the future, human civilization is now being called upon to amend its cultural misbehaviors. In the profound words offered by Tim Kastelle, Innovation Management professor at the University of Queensland, "To Create the Future, We Must Understand the Past."[51]

I believe that to gain the insight we seek, we must actually go back over four billion years to the origin of life. The first living cells, *prokaryotes* (i.e., bacteria) and *archaea* (single-celled organisms living in environmental extremes) were endowed with a vital life force referred to as the *Biological Imperative,* which represents the drive to survive. This imperative programs organisms with two main behavioral directives: (1) the survival of the individual, and (2) the survival of the species. In the individual, the imperative engages an unconscious drive that causes organisms to breathe, drink water, seek nourishment and protect themselves. Even the most primitive bacterium, when threatened, will seek every means at its disposal to survive.

The imperative also includes the fundamental drive to reproduce, the mechanism that sustains the perpetuity of the species. In higher forms of multicellular organisms, the necessary reproductive strategy is manifest through the mating interaction between female and male individuals.

At mating time for bees and ants, a fleet of drones fly into the air and compete to see which individual will successfully mate with the virgin queen. Please note that the term "compete" is predicated on the original definition of *competition*: "To strive together." Drone competition is not a battle based on winners and losers, it is the equivalent of a sporting event to see which drone is the most powerful, which one represents the individual with the most fit genes to support the viability of the community's next generation.

However, the concept of competition takes on a profoundly different meaning among male mammals. Rather than striving together, mammalian competition is expressed as a "battle" to defeat or establish superiority over others, a challenge that is predicated on winners and losers. In chimpanzee troops, when a younger male defeats a former alpha male, he even kills the juvenile progeny of the former leader to ensure that the new alpha male's genes determine the fate of the tribe's next generation.

Unfortunately, the biological imperative in higher mammals goes beyond the drive to survive to include the quest for personal empowerment. Originally, kings ruled as alpha males because of their physical courage and bravery in fighting off challengers to their throne. However, subsequent heirs of the king maintained control of their community, not so much through physical prowess, but through the empowerment afforded by controlling the land's *resources*. Leaders with resources could buy allegiance by offering a share of their resources in exchange for their physically empowered rivals' services as guards and military personnel. Females in these societies were more attracted to those with resources, choosing them over individuals that were simply more physically endowed. Driven by her biological imperative, a woman sought to bond with males whose resources were more likely to support her reproductive function in securing the fate of her offspring, and thus the perpetuity of the species.

Over time, evolution led to yet another source of personal empowerment . . . *knowledge.* An ancient proverb emphasizes that having more knowledge offers more control over one's future. This truth was first immortalized in the 1597 edition of *Meditationes Sacrae* by Sir Francis Bacon, *"Ipsa scientia potestas est"* [Knowledge itself is power]. Subsequently, the Church of Rome capitalized on the empowerment offered by knowledge when it declared that it represented Infallible Knowledge, a claim that simply translates as *absolute power.* The fact that knowledge held sway over the powers provided by both physical prowess and the control of resources was demonstrated in the behavior of kings who bowed before and kissed the ring of the Pope.

Infallible knowledge empowered the Church to became Western Civilization's "truth provider." The knowledge it offered shaped cultural behavior for a thousand-year reign in a civilization referred to as Judeo-Christian monotheism. Infallible knowledge ultimately became a dangerous and limiting belief that prevented the world from gaining new awareness beyond that provided in the Bible or by the edicts of the Church.

One example of the Church's destructive infallible knowledge is the biblical story in Genesis of Adam and Eve in the Garden of Eden that taught believers that humans were created separately from the origin of Nature and were given dominion over life by God. This perception has significantly contributed to today's mass extinction in that it acknowledged the rights of religious observers to wantonly desecrate the planet's web of life.

To perpetuate its claim of infallibility, the Church invoked the deadly Inquisition, a "kangaroo court" that jailed, tortured and killed dissenters labelled as heretics. In addition to heretics killed in the Spanish Inquisition, it is believed that the Church systematically put to death over a million "nonbelievers," including Gnostics, Protestants, Jews, Muslims, and indigenous South American natives. It is still hard to conceive how the Church, professing to represent the Love in the teachings of Jesus the Christ, could not only kill heretics in His name, but also convince their followers to cheer the burning at the stake of 40 to 50 thousand women deemed to be witches. Thus is the power of "fallible" knowledge.

The Church's claim of infallible knowledge was broken in 1543 with the deathbed release of *De revolutionibus orbium coelestium* (*On the Revolutions of the Celestial Spheres*) by Nicholas Copernicus, a Catholic priest, astronomer, and medical doctor. Copernicus's research revealed the earth was a planet in orbit around a central sun. This new knowledge successfully challenged the Bible's story of the earth being the center of God's firmament. The release of Copernicus's book on the day of his death is recognized as the origin date of the Modern Scientific Revolution.

While Copernicus undermined the claim of infallible knowledge in the mid-1500s, the Church managed to rule civilization until Darwin's *Origin of Species* was published in 1859. It was shortly after this time that the Judeo-Christian monotheism civilization ended, and the new truths offered by science provided for the current civilization designated as "scientific materialism."

During Western civilization's era of scientific materialism, cultural norms were primarily derived from the principles and philosophy of modern science. The most influential principles shaping scientific philosophy were those promulgated by Newtonian physics and Darwinian evolution theory. While the advances offered by science in the last 150 years border on the miraculous, its failures have significantly contributed to the current mass extinction event that in the end, could conceivably terminate the existence of human civilization.

It is a truism that "Knowledge is power." However, the inverse of that proverb, "A lack of knowledge is a lack of power," may be more relevant when we consider "misperceptions" as truths. This is particularly significant in regard to the cultural consequences of misperceptions inherent in Newtonian and Darwinian philosophy.

Newtonian physics subdivided the universe into two separate realms: the material, physical realm and an invisible energy realm. A basic assumption implied in Newtonian physics is the notion that matter can affect matter, which led to the presumption that a body made out of matter can only be influenced by other forms of matter. This is why conventional allopathic medicine relies on prescribing pharmaceutical drugs in managing healthcare issues. Of course, this notion immediately falls apart when considering that one-third or more of medical healings are attributed to the consciousness mediated *placebo effect*.

Perhaps of more significance is that in a matter-centric universe, the implied separation of matter-energy realms challenges the existence and influence of spirituality (i.e., energy) in human life. Between 1851 and 2000, statistics reveal that the impact of civilization's era of scientific materialism resulted in a steady and consistent decline in religiosity. For example, in a journal article entitled "Christianity in Britain, R. I. P." author Steve Bruce writes: "Unless long-stable trends are reversed, major British (Christian) denominations will cease to exist by 2030."[52]

Similarly, two fundamental misperceptions propagated by neo-Darwinian evolution theory have also had a negative influence on the fate of civilization. The bio-mechanical version of the theory emphasizes that evolution is driven by a two-step process: (1) Random (accidental) genetic mutations initiate the evolution process; followed by (2) Natural selection determines the fate of the mutated gene. If the mutation is beneficial it will be propagated in future generations; if the mutation is detrimental to the organism's viability, it will be eliminated by not being passed on to future generations.

One problem lies in the first assumption that mutations are random, accidental events, which means that by definition evolution is driven by chance. A mechanism based on "chance" profoundly influences the answer to the perennial question, "Why are we here?" It would mean that evolution is a crapshoot, the result of luck derived from thousands of shakes in a game of genetic "dice." Our existence would represent an accident, with no intended purpose or design for humanity. Thus Darwinian theory functionally disconnects human evolution from nature and the web of life, with much the same consequences as the biblical story in Genesis.

The second disempowering misperception implied in neo-Darwinism is the concept of *genetic determinism,* the notion that heredity controls our physical, behavioral, and emotional character. While science has since revised this misperception, the public is still imbued with the belief that their fate is predetermined in the genome passed down through their parents. This misperception is disempowering because it can make people think they are "victims" of their genes over which they have no control. Once they perceive themselves as victims, people give up authority to manage their lives and seek empowerment through medical practitioners and prescription drugs. However, this trade-off comes with a high price since the practice of allopathic medicine is the third leading cause of death in the United States.[53]

Welcome to the Future: The consciousness and behavioral character of the era of *Scientific Materialism* is devoid of spirituality and deference to Mother Nature, and, as a consequence, it has fomented the 6th mass extinction event. We have hit the proverbial wall, for the chaos we are now experiencing sounds the death knell for human civilization. But it is crisis that precipitates evolution and we can survive by changing our current way of life! And new knowledge provided by quantum physics and epigenetics illuminate an opportunity to create a new, sustainable version of civilization.

Conventional Newtonian physics that emphasized that the universe is subdivided into two separate realms, matter and energy, was officially invalidated in 1927 when the world was introduced to the new science of quantum physics. Quantum physicists revealed that atoms, the building blocks of matter, are derived from invisible energy vortices resembling "nanotornedos." The new physics actually demonstrates that the universe is comprised of only one realm . . . energy.

While energy fields are invisible, the reason we can see what appears to be matter is a trick of light. When photons from a light source hit an atom's condensed energy field, the photons are deflected and can be visualized by our eyes or photographic media. Consequently, the physical appearance of matter is simply an illusion derived from reflected photons. This insight led Einstein to acknowledge that "Reality is merely an illusion, albeit a persistent one."

An atom's spinning energy vortex generates a force field. When we push on an atom, the resistant force field "pushes back." This action produces the sensation that matter has a physical quality. In ascribing a physical character to our perception of matter, we incorrectly perceive that matter is characterized by defined physical borders that separate one form of matter from another form of matter. This leads to the illusion that material objects are separate individual entities.

The nature of this misperception is dispelled when we recognize that an atom's energy generates a field resembling ripples in a pond. A useful analogy to consider is the action of raindrops creating ripples in a pool of water. Each raindrop represents a spinning atom, while the radiating ripples it creates represent emitted electromagnetic energy waves produced by the nano-tornedo energy vortex at the core of each atom.

The significant insight offered by this analogy is that the ripples derived from each drop of water, across the whole surface of the pool, are all interconnected and entangled. The awareness of matter's radiating energy fields reveals that our own personal energy field is inextricably entangled with every other human's field, as well as with every other material object's field in the universe. Likewise, the energy ripples from each atom comprising our perception of matter are entangled with radiating energy waves emitted by every other atom in the universe! The universe is a singularity of energy and cannot be subdivided into separate "physical" elements. While Newtonian science emphasizes individuality, quantum physics emphasizes unity. All is one!

A principle of quantum physics emphasizes that invisible energy fields are the sole governing agency of the particle (i.e., our perception of matter). A simple definition for an energy field is: *Invisible moving forces that influence the physical world.*

It is not a coincidence that spirit can also be defined as: *Invisible moving forces that influence the physical world.* Field = Spirit! The principles of quantum physics unite modern science with the insights offered by ancient spirituality.

Quantum physics has proven to be the most valid and truthful of all sciences on planet Earth. A fundamental tenet of quantum physics is that consciousness, as an energy field, creates our experience of reality. An article by physicist Richard Conn Henry in the most prestigious scientific journal, *Nature*, concludes: "The Universe is immaterial—it's mental and spiritual. Live and enjoy."[54]

The new awareness provided by quantum physics offers civilization an opportunity to create a new sustainable world. Similarly, the new science of epigenetics offers individuals an understanding of their personal creative power. In contrast to the conventional belief that genes control biology, epigenetics emphasizes that the environment, and more specifically, our perception of the environment, controls genetic expression.[55]

In the era of genetic determinism, genes were invoked as the primary cause of disease. However, recent data reveals that genes are responsible for causing about 1 percent of disease.[56] Up to 90 percent of the majority of illnesses, including heart disease, cancer, and diabetes, are directly due to the influence of stress, an expression of consciousness over which we actually have control.[57]

I can almost hear your response challenging the assertion that personal consciousness is responsible for manifesting problems and health issues that plague your life. Why would anyone knowingly do this? As described in *The Biology of Belief*, the action of the mind is the source of consciousness that shapes the character of our lives.[58] Functionally, the character of the mind's consciousness is derived from the integration of two functional subdivisions of the nervous system, the conscious mind and the subconscious mind.

The creative conscious mind, influenced by our personal spiritual energy field, represents the source of our wishes, desires, and aspirations. In contrast, the subconscious mind, resembling a computer's hard drive, is a programmable database of downloaded life experiences. The primary programs downloaded into the subconscious mind are simply acquired by observing the behavior of parents, siblings and community members during the first seven years of life. Unfortunately, the majority of subconscious programs we download are limiting, disempowering and self-sabotaging behaviors.

We would love to believe that our behavior is derived from the conscious mind's positive traits; however, psychologists have determined that 95 percent of our cognitive activity comes from subconscious programs.[59] The reason behind this fact is that 95 percent of the day the attention of the conscious mind is focused inwardly, engaged in the process of thinking. While the conscious mind is busy, the subconscious mind steps in as an autopilot to control cognitive activity. A conscious mind preoccupied in thought does not observe nor become aware of the often destructive subconscious behaviors they are engaging in.

While this is a relatively new scientific insight, the Jesuits have been aware of this fact for over 400 years, as attested to by their claim, "Give me a child for the first seven years and I will give you the man."

To conclude, we are personally responsible for the character of our life and health, although most may not have been aware of that fact until they understood the content in the previous paragraph. What would life be like if we did not default to subconscious control? As those who have fallen in love and experienced the happiness and robust health that is the amazing result of staying "mindful" and not defaulting to subconscious control, it would be a honeymoon![60] (ref: The Honeymoon Effect).

For most, the joy of the honeymoon is short lived. Life's responsibilities inevitably require the conscious mind to engage in thinking, which leads to a return of subconscious control of cognitive processing. But ponder this thought: What would be the consequence of rewriting limiting subconscious programs so they reflect the wishes and desires of the conscious mind? The answer: A honeymoon experience for every day of your life, whether you are operating from either the conscious or the unconscious mind!

Evolution—by the People, for the Planet: The revised knowledge provided by quantum biophysics and epigenetics affirms our role as creators and this awareness can usher in a new version of civilization resembling the honeymoon we all seek. Civilization, now in transition, is moving out of a world in which we perceive ourselves to be "victims" of life to a new version of reality wherein we actively exercise our powers as conscious "creators."

As one version of civilization ends, a new one begins. Evolution does not "throw out the baby with the bath water," it is a process of carrying forward civilization's good traits while revising behaviors that are not beneficial. Civilization is actively reviewing the good and the bad aspects of human history in order to redefine and evolve humanity and its relationship with Mother Nature. Movements such as *Me Too*, *Black Lives Matter*, and *Environmental Green* are bringing to light civilization's current dysfunctions.

By revising our role in life, we can actively participate in empowering civilization to transition into a world based on Love and Harmony. In the process, we must honor and extend the wonderful supportive behaviors that have historically enhanced civilization, such as a focus on family and community health and well-being. Because the collective amplitude of a large community sharing the same consciousness can profoundly change the world. Through conscious evolution, we will all be able to experience Heaven on Earth!

++++

The Japanese Perspective on the Approach to a Better World: An Inner Dialogue

by Tomoyo Nonaka

If Leonardo da Vinci were alive today, what would he tell us?

We have overcome storms like the plague in the 15th century many times in our history. Now more than two decades into the 21st century, we are again smitten by a pandemic—this time from the COVID-19 virus. We are aware of how appalling it is. As I write this, the number of confirmed cases of the disease is over 122 million. The number who have died is nearly 2.7 million, and the figures will grow.

But we've learned that when the plague of the 15th century was over, the Renaissance began to bloom. By destroying the two biggest social powers—the Church and the Feudal Lords—which nobody could ever believe could be crushed—people have come to gain their own social and political status as citizens.

Yes, and now it's our turn!

We should recognize that this is our golden opportunity to shift the world for good. It is our mission to lead the shift as a member of the WorldShift team formed by Ervin Laszlo.

It is a great honor that Ervin entrusted me with the task of writing about the approach to a new era from the Eastern perspective. Since I am not a physicist, economist, anthropologist, or a scholar and have limited space to express my views, please allow my contribution to be sketched as my own thoughts. As I engage in the subject of the Eastern Perspective, I will focus on Japanese culture and its present condition.

Watch out! Just who or what is the enemy we all face?

Historically speaking, it is proper to say that this was after the Industrial Revolution, but especially for the Japanese experience, let me focus on the period after World War II. Most social systems (not only in economics and politics but also in education) were structured in order to make our defeated land and society more civilized, better than before. Our slogan was "Catch up with America! Overtake America!" People worked so hard that being called an "economic animal" sounded like a compliment. Why not work still harder?

The more you devote your time for to the company, the wealthier you can be. The more money you get, the happier life you can have! This was our social belief at that time. We call those years "the Showa miracle (昭和)" of high-economic growth (1955–73). We became the second richest country on this planet. People had no ears or eyes for the warning of the Club of Rome about the Limits to Growth!

After getting past the 1st and 2nd oil shocks and overcoming heavy pollution by establishing new environmental technologies, we have come into the "Reiwa years" (令和), the lost 30 years (1989–2019). During this low economic growth period, the so-called Finance Capitalism Storm has affected not only Japan but the whole world.

No matter how nice (or naïve? or insensitive? or money addicted) we ordinary Japanese people have been, we doubted whether this financial capitalism-oriented society would be appropriate to create human happiness. And then, over the last decade since the Japanese government launched the Quantitative Easing policy (printing money) in an astronomical dimension (the leaders themselves said so!) and sustaining (buying stocks! even with our pension funds), the Tokyo Stock Exchange Market, in other words, the Japanese economy, "looked" to be still in a good shape. But I believe it's not a healthy capitalism at all. The stock holders become much richer, and now that COVID-19 has hit, ordinary people became much poorer. Although in the 1960s some opinion polls found over 95 percent of the people recognized themselves as middle class, now Japan has become divided country. We have learned the good-looking economic figure and chasing more money do not always lead us toward true well-being.

Monotheism or Polytheism?

When we talk about the difference between the East and the West in general, there are some points that cannot be avoided. One of them is about Religion which we all know is such a complicated and delicate matter. So as an amateur, let me try to make some points that are both bold and simple.

We Japanese are often said to be an irreligious people, although in Kyoto there are lots of beautiful shrines and temples. Sorry to say it, but this is a misunderstanding. Of course, there are many pious Buddhists, Christians, Muslims, and other groups of faith here in Japan, it is true we actually have no particular national religion. But we do have 八百万神 (*Yao Yorozu no Kami*). "Yao Yorozu" means eight million, and "Kami" means God. Yes, we have more than eight million Gods in Japan. So aren't we religious! In other words, we believe and can feel Gods in trees, rocks, moon, sun, and even in clouds and winds—all around us in nature, and we put our hands together and turn toward them to express our appreciation.

You can call this as a kind of polytheism, but more in particular, it should be recognized as a social custom or a cultural behavior established in daily life for a long time, rather than as a Religion. (It has been about 16,000 years since we've had such assimilation into nature, society, and lifestyles.) It was 縄文時代 = the Johmon Era.

When recognizing ourselves, our existence is in the bosom of Nature, our sense is that we are not living creatures, but creatures which are allowed to live. By whom? Jesus? Buddha? . . . No: We are allowed to live by the grace of the Gods of Nature!

My esteemed mentor and friend Dr. K. Murakami who created the world's first Rice Genome analysis told me, "Our work was, yes, so miraculously done! But Tomoyo, the real miracle worker is the creator of the original genome. Who do you think created it?" He called that creator "Something Great." I was so impressed to hear this expression from such a brilliant scientist.

For the Japanese, nature is not the environment surrounding us but is like our mother's womb. We are naturally, inherently, inside of nature. We feel ourselves in that womb.

European philosophy and religion, in the monotheistic form, seems to come from awakening, from confronting nature. In short, a hierarchy is created. God is first on the top; under him are the humans, then nature. But in Japan, the top is nature viewed in the form of eight million Gods who nurture us.

I remember a story my friend told me. In Europe in the old days when people faced a black and deep forest, they felt fear. They decided to pioneer and cultivate this wilderness by cutting trees to bring sunlight for enlightenment, overcoming what they considered the dark evilness. This created a "cultured" society. On the contrary, people in Japan in the old days went deep into the woods not with fear but with joy and respect. They found big trees and rocks and made them into Gods to worship as the local guardian deities. These polytheism cultures are called 古神道 (*Ko Shintoh*). The last characters mean ancient Shintoh (神道). The forests with *Torii* (the gate pole towards the sacred precincts) are called 鎮守の森 (*Ching Ju no Mori*). They were all over Japan. These aspects of nature might be very powerful if applied in the West when confronted with environmental problems in the future. In other words, the key shift to establish them is to be more humble and modest and respectful toward the earth's natural elements.

Will the Renaissance of the 21st Century come from Japan?

Going through post WWII economic capitalism, especially in urban areas, people have been throwing off everything of Japanese taste with joy in order to follow and try to attain the

Western, and more exactly, the American way of life. Sadly enough, our humbleness and reverence for Nature was also flung away.

Actually, we have already experienced such drastic social behavior in middle of the 19th century, after 300 years of the Shoguns' Edo era as we moved toward the Meiji Restoration era. Samurais cut off the Chonmage topknot hairstyle of the privileged to make a short "Lincoln" cut. It is also in our "nature," is it not? We have strong stomachs to secrete tough cultural digestive enzymes once we have made up our minds to survive on this small island, where there is no escape besides the ocean in which we can submerge until we die.

One thing I would like to share here is that we Japanese people are not bad at shifting our value-standards. Once we have the confidence that it is the right direction for a better life, we just go forward.

Now let's go fast forward

After being the second richest country in the world, some of the wealth bubbles did pop off and were levelled by the Lehman shock. But these economic ups and downs were within one and the same game, with the same rules of the market applying to them.

But this is not the case anymore. The rules of the game themselves have changed.

Now we should recognize the truth that we are in the middle of a radical planetary social shift, whether we like it or not. This is due to the appearance of cutting-edge information and communication technologies (ICTs). Sooner or later the challenge of achieving well-being will not be one of governmental regulations, but of the ICTs. It is going to be another game.

Curiosity and imagination are timeless sources of energy!

The word "planetary" reminds me of four gentlemen: Buckminster Fuller, H. Marshall McLuhan, Joseph J. Campbell, and James Lovelock. As a susceptible youth, I found their words deeply resonating in me at that time. "Spaceship Earth," "the Media is the Message," "Global Village," "Gaia Theory," and so on. Those words were wake-up calls and made us, especially the younger generation, open our eyes to the Universe and gave us perspective to look down and understand the things that happened on this small planet named Earth. These were my golden 60s and 70s!

Now in the 21st century, the pandemic created a similar but much deeper awakening. I could not help going back to my library and look for the small book by Erwin Schrödinger *What is Life*, which I read in the 80s in my grad school days when I was majoring in journalism. I remember clearly it was so difficult to understand, but it was so impressive because it did connect my perspective of the universe with the quantum world and gave me the sense of being alive. Here I do not have enough space to write about it, but the point catalyzed in my heart is that we live our lives within the frame of Universal energy.

Of course, I also picked up another of my most important books from my shelves to read again: *CosMos* by Ervin Laszlo and Jude Currivan. These are all highly recommended readings for creating a new paradigm of well-being.

Vaccination for the spirit?

The media and politicians are talking loudly about "which vaccine is best"—and about how inoculation should be effected. Indeed, this is urgent! We need to find out how to eradicate the pandemic. But at the same time, we should not forget that there is also another important issue we have to deal with. We've learned that in the 14th and 15th centuries people could bravely confront their situation and overcome suffering. They might have thought that attempting to do so is as impossible as turning the sky and the earth upside down. But they went ahead, and they did succeed. Why? Because they had their own hopes and dreams freed from the feudal bondage. While overcoming the plague, they did not forget to seek their well-being.

Why not us? What is our new well-being? Again, find out first: What is the challenge?

As we humans have been trying hard to get MORE in all the aspects of our lives, the power of MORE has been, for better or worse, so powerful that things have become very complicated in all aspects of our life. We live in an intricate intertwined society.

Can you point to two words that come to your mind?

Yes. It may sound strange, but the first word we should be careful to use is "diversity." This word has become popular, and that is good. It knocked down divisive thinking in society.

Communist or capitalist? Democrat or Republican? Male or female? Rich or poor? And so on. Ensuring diversity, we would be compassionate and tolerant and accept differences. But at the same time, it seems to me that our mind and our ability to sense dangers and challenges are melting down. Somehow we got entangled, and somehow we got into a spider web where words are too facile to be useful.

The other term is SDGs (Sustainable Development Goals). This is also okay. Better than nothing. As a universal common measurement and language, it is good. But we should be very careful. It can distract people's eyes from knowing and searching for the real cause of the origins of the problems. We have no time to be just a "greenwasher."

Einstein: No problem can be solved at the level of consciousness that created it!

The pandemic today tells us there is no difference whether rich or poor, man or woman, prime minister or king—everyone can get infected. The virus does not care how much money you have, the color of your skin, and what the borders are of your country. The pandemic reminds me of the issue of global warming. But when COVID-19 proved to be invisible with no smell or sound, a micro-tiny bit of an existent entered the world, the world stopped! We stopped! No business. No flights. No going out to eat. No events. And just stay HOME with your family. In the twinkling of an eye, the water in Venice becomes clean, and Dolphins come back, and the air in India is so clean that the Himalayas could be seen.

It proved to us that our value-standards for happiness (directing business, going around by plane, shopping for things from far-away countries . . .) no longer do justice to our life. We saw the standards should be shifted to maintain a clean environment. Is this an extreme requirement? No, not at all. COVID-19 taught us this. You can stay home with your beloved family and in this way we can live. This means first that we should focus on our own local community and rebuild it so it is sustainable. Yes, back to the original behavior on this planet of the Earth. It's not going back to Woodstock. There are lots of ways to shift our value-standards and to start a new way of living.

No Being, No Well-Being!

During the pandemic, we did freeze. Why? Because people were scared. After the terrifying symptoms, we finally recognized what the most important thing in our lives is. Living. We want to live and not to die. We found the real culprit who scared us. It's Us! Thus, "life" and "being alive" is the answer. In Japanese we call it 命 (*Inochi*), which has many deep and subtle and complex meanings . . . but this time, let me go on. Well-being from now on cannot be realized without establishing how to live a healthier and safer life in "our" area. Only then can it be realized on the planetary level.

Could we do this without Big Money?

Finally, we have woken up to find out the true nature of our existence on this planet. We share the same moment and watch together the same scenes on the internet just like watching a live show on TV. We finally feel the truth of "We are in the same boat."

We are connected through living and breathing not only with other human beings but with all living creatures. Look at your goldfish in the bowl. Water for them is as air is for us. Our air is provided and cleaned by the trees and oceans that we have been destroying now for a long time, believing it will make us wealthy, comfortable, and create "well-being," as we are driven by the energy of our quest for MORE.

Money is great and powerful, but it is only the instrument, and not the goal and the objective of our lives. We sometimes mistake the means for the goal. Then we lose what is truly important: Our most important and valuable thing that is our "being alive."

"All's fair in love and war" is an old saying, and it could have been changed in the name of Globalization into "All's fair when making money."

I am not naïve enough to proclaim that money is evil or useless, but I want to affirm that it's only the instrument, the means to an end. The question is how to use it, and for what purpose. It could powerfully create new well-being in the world. When I became CEO of Sanyo Electric in 2005 for creating a new vision, "Think Gaia," for the company, we were able to make a washing machine without wasting water and made other world-first ecological products. Although we created many Think Gaia products, I resigned. This was more than a decade before the "Lehman Shock," and at the time nobody in the financial field, the investment bankers, securities brokers and others, cared about nature and the future of this planet. They cared only about profit. Their purposes, goals, careers, hobbies—the acts of their entire existence—were dedicated to the goal of having More Money.

Can We Go from Money-Centric Capitalism to Ordinary Citizen-Capitalism?

The social systems based on our financial leaders' money-centric capitalism is so strong that we believed we could not rebel against it. It was all-mighty, and we believed so without a shadow of doubt.

But it is time to stand up and act! The time has come!

Let me make it clear that we should stand up with a "Smile"! Fighting against others and hurting or killing the enemy is not our way. Our standing up is not to cause harm to any living creature.

Eight million Gods would be with us!

The territory of Japan is about the same size as just one state in the USA: California! Such a small country! And with 120 million people inhabiting it, fortunately, nearly 70 percent of the remaining usable land is forest.

Added to this, in Japan, there are so many words starting with "Ki" (the character 気) that is equivalent to the Chinese character "Qui" and when combined with other verbs has meanings of air, atmosphere, flavor, energy, as well as meaning thoughts, feelings, heart, spirit, will, and even consciousness. Japanese people have long known and felt that all natural elements of our earth are connecting us with universal energy. Actually there are some 武士道 (*Bushido*) martial artists who can defeat their opponents solely with their Ki as the weapon. My Karate master, Kenji Ushirom is at the top of this field. He describes Ki as "depth of thought, the consciousness that enables simultaneous, multidimensional movement" by connecting with Universal energy at the quantum level.

It is my strong belief and hope that the island called Japan can contribute to the new paradigm for a better life for all living creatures. Our challenge is to shift our standard of value from Money to Being (being alive = *Inochi*).

In this regard, I want to share with you the chart that our members of the WorldShift Japan Chapter of the Club of Budapest international network made into our branding-icon. I believe that sharing this chart with as many people as possible would help us realize that making this shift by every one of us matters.

We don't need one great Leonardo, but ordinary citizens who connect together and create a better world: An Era of Well-Being.

This is my Shift. The standard of value changes from Money to Inochi

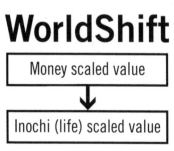

++++

The God-Redefinition Approach
to an Era of Well-Being

by Neale Donald Walsch

For years, we have received spiritual guidance to be "in this world, but not of it." It's been widely advised (in those exact words, actually) from the time of Jesus and suggested in more general terms as a workable *modus operandi* by the elders and philosophers of our species from very early on in our jointly undertaken Earthly adventures.

In more recent times this notion has been reinforced by the repeated reminders of our contemporary spiritual teachers that we are, in fact, eternal metaphysical entities, and that our purpose on Earth has to do with the soul's agenda, not the desires of the body or the excursions of the mind.

So now, a question.

If we really are spiritual beings living eternally and serving the Agenda of the Soul, why should we pay particular attention to our physical life—much less place the enormous amount of focus on it that most people do?

What's the purpose of continuing our millennia-long struggle to create possibilities for heading toward a better world if we are not even *of* this world?

Are we wasting our time with our forever-ongoing explorations of what we can do in this physical life to create a better world? If not, what would it take to produce the outcome?

Our species has been trying to figure this out for 50 millennia. Not 50 decades, or 50 centuries, but 50 *millennia*. This endless search has resulted in over 4,300 religions being practiced on this planet today, with the followers of each feeling deeply assured that they have found the answer.

Alas, the proof is not in the pudding. With all of this thinking and all of these theologies endlessly making efforts to show us "the way," we still, as a species, find ourselves unable to take the most elementary steps toward becoming an advanced civilization. Like just getting along, for instance. (There has been armed conflict somewhere on this planet for 92 percent of recorded history.) Or simply feeding ourselves. (Over 840 million people—one out of eight of us—go to bed hungry every night, and more than 650 of our children die of starvation every hour.) And the sad evidence of our inability to find an answer to the human dilemma doesn't stop there. One member of our species commits suicide every 40 seconds. In 2017, just under 465,000 of us were murdered.

All of this has for years led me to wonder: Could it be that, in our search for a solution, we are simply looking in the wrong place? Is it possible that there is something we don't fully understand about God, about life, and about ourselves, *the understanding of which would change everything?*

I'm going to suggest that the answer is yes. And I'm going to propose that what we don't understand fully is how to meld the physical aspect of our lives with the metaphysical reality of our true identity. Most of us don't even embrace our true identity, much less seek to meld it into our experience.

To get to the heart of the matter, we would benefit enormously today from placing the primary emphasis of our thinking not on what we are *doing*, but on what we are *being*. I hold this idea because I observe that it is from what I call "beingness" that all "doingness" emerges. It is what we are being in response to people, circumstances, and events (are we being fearful, are we being angry, are we being understanding and forgiving?) that determines how we act. And how we are being is determined to a huge extent by what we believe.

Therefore, if we truly wish to change how we are proceeding on this human journey, I want to suggest that we're going to have to change our beliefs. And specifically, our beliefs about the deity.

Why? Because so many people model their behavior on their belief about the behavior of God.

It is, of course, true that some people don't believe there is a God. Yet the millions in this group are dramatically affected by the even larger number of those who firmly do believe in a deity. It's neither "right" nor "wrong" to belong to either group—but the second group certainly does affect the first, and winds up generating behaviors reflected by most of humanity.

Anthropological surveys have consistently shown that eight out of ten people believe in a "Higher Power." And the power of all those beliefs about that higher power demonstrably influences many people's day-to-day decisions.

Those who believe that God is judgmental will likely be judgmental. Those who believe that God condemns people will likely condemn others. Those who believe that God punishes people will likely punish others. And (perhaps most impact-fully) those who believe that God is separate from them will likely feel separate from God and embrace a Separation Theology. This is a theology that says "I am 'over here' and God is 'over there,' and never the 'twain shall meet—until I die and God decides whether I have been good enough to come back 'home' and to be back with God 'over there.'"

Now that wouldn't be so bad if it started and ended there. The world's major religions would get to teach what they teach, and the world's people would get to believe what they believe. But the problem with a Separation Theology is that it produces a Separation Cosmology—that is, a cosmological way of look-ing at all of Life, which holds that everything is separate from everything else.

That wouldn't be so bad either, if that's all there was to it, but the problem with a Separation Cosmology is that it pro-duces a Separation Psychology, meaning a personal thinking about the human psyche that says everyone is alone, separate from everything and everyone else.

Even that might be at some level workable for a species if that were the only outcome, but the challenge is that a Separation Psychology produces a Separation Sociology, a way of socializ-ing the human species which creates groups and nationalities and memberships that declare their interests to all be separate.

This is where things start getting dangerous, because a Separation Sociology too often produces a Separation Pathol-ogy—pathological behaviors of self-destruction, engaged in individually and collectively, and evidenced everywhere on our planet throughout human history.

So we see that a theology produces our views of cosmology, which produces our views of psychology, which produces our views of sociology, which produces our pathology.

I am suggesting here that our ongoing dysfunction as a civilization goes back to what we believe about Our Maker. Here's what I want to offer, then: A solution to the problem of how to create an era of well-being is to come up with a brand-new definition of God.

Our old definition of God has led to the governments of many countries intentionally killing people as a way of teaching people that intentionally killing people is not okay. It has led to many groups using attacks against other groups to show that attacks against groups are not okay. It has led to people of particular genders, particular nationalities, particular skin colors, and particular sexual realities suffering blatant discrimination as other people apply what they believe are correct and proper guiding principles for our human species.

All of this is, after all, only about God-fearing people obeying the God of whom they are afraid.

Yet what if God is not to be feared? What if we could not justify our most unloving behaviors with others (judging, condemning, punishing them) by pointing to how our deity behaves with us?

My experience is that very few people think about the world's problems in these terms. As a result, we have been creating life on Earth without seeing the direct connection between our beliefs and our behaviors, between our spiritual lives and our physical lives. We have been generating physical outcomes (wars, poverty, the suffering of millions, our current alienations) without an awareness of their metaphysical causes.

And the biggest metaphysical cause? Our belief in separation. The 80 percent of us who believe in God believe that God is something *other than us*. And so we keep trying to solve the world's problems at every level except the level at which the problems exist.

We try to solve the problems as if they were political problems, but that hasn't worked. We pass resolutions and sign agreements and vote for changes, but the same problems continue to arise, millennia after millennia.

So then we try to solve the problems as if they were economic problems, but that hasn't worked, either. We throw money at them, or withhold money from them, as in the form of sanctions, but the same problems continue to arise, millennia after millennia.

So then we say, "Ah, these must be military problems!" and we shoot bullets at them and drop bombs on them, replacing the rocks and spears and swords of earlier times. But that also hasn't worked, and the same problems continue to arise, even into the New Millennium.

What humanity does not seem to understand is that its basic problem is not a political problem, it is not an economic problem, and it is not a military problem. The problem facing humanity is a *spiritual* problem—and it can only be solved by spiritual means.

The problem has to do with how we believe we are supposed to act with each other—and this belief, to reiterate with emphasis, is based on how eight out of ten of us believe that God acts with us.

The solution, then, is to dramatically alter our thinking regarding the model we have been using to construct our behaviors. And in this, we don't have a moment to lose.

Our governments have ignored enough warnings about our many environmental crises to take us to the brink of irreparable damage. Our races and religions have made enough statements about their superiority and the inferiority of others to produce a level of group alienation and individual antagonism that is making the mutual meeting of challenges increasingly difficult. And we already know that some nations have enough nuclear weapons stockpiled to blow the planet to bits.

It's going to take a Revolution of Beliefs if we wish to truly create an era of well-being tomorrow.

I have a hypothesis to offer around that. I have an idea that humanity would hugely benefit at this stage if we could come up with an idea about the higher power that all the world's religions and cultures could agree on. This idea could then become the basis for a New Global Ethic to be applied to politics, economics, social interactions, and our spiritual expressions.

I am honing in now on that new definition of God that I spoke of earlier. I am going to suggest that we explore an idea about God that defines the higher power not as a larger-than-life celestial being in the sky who grants or fails to grant our wishes (depending upon all sorts of unclear factors) but rather as a self-conscious, self-aware, self-activating energy—what I call the Essential Essence—that emanates from a single source and embeds its presence in every sentient life form.

I want to further suggest that life forms experience this presence as a *feeling*. It is a very particular and one-of-a-kind feeling that we might describe with a variety of terms, such as warmth, oneness, complete understanding, absolute acceptance, and—to roll it all into one word—love.

Now this may not be as simplistic as it might sound, because in the use of that last word I am referring to a very specific and particular kind of love.

I am referring to what I call Pure Love.

This is the new definition of God that I suggest could, if we embraced it, change the world.

Pure Love is an energy that comes free of any obligation. It needs, asks, expects, and demands nothing in return.

You are keenly aware of it when you have received Pure Love from another. And you feel it deeply when you have expressed it as well. Perhaps you have expressed it with a baby. Or with a pet. Or even with another fully-grown human being. There is absolutely no mistaking the feeling of Pure Love when it moves through you, in you, as you.

So when I think of how we could each help create possibilities for a better tomorrow, I think not of what each of us could Do, but what each of us could Be. I think of how the physical and the metaphysical could meld, giving meaning to our outward experience by giving expression to our inward identity as an aspect, or individuation, of divinity.

Many folks have a difficult time thinking of themselves in this way. But I see our relationship to God as the same as the relationship of a wave to the ocean. The wave is not other than the ocean, nor is it separate from the ocean. It is an expression *of* the ocean, and when its expression is complete, it recedes back into the ocean, whence it came.

So what I have come to call The God Solution is our defining God as Pure Love, and our identifying, personally, with that Essential Essence.

And I have discovered a tool that I have found to be remarkably effective in determining if Pure Love is the ethic being adopted and projected by a group or individual. I simply ask myself a question regarding what I am observing at any given moment: *Does this feel like Pure Love?*

For instance, I might ask myself, when I hear of a person being put to death as punishment for what he has done, *Does it feel like Pure Love is being expressed*? Is this behavior modeling God?

When I hear that some people are not allowed to vote, not allowed to drive, not allowed to attend school, or not allowed to hold a particular job, because they are not male, *does it feel like Pure Love is being expressed*? Is this behavior modeling God?

When I hear that rental of an apartment, or the purchase of a wedding cake, or the issuing of a marriage license, has been refused to a couple because they are the same sex, *does it feel like Pure Love is being expressed*? Is this behavior modeling God?

I am not unaware that there are some people who would say "yes." That is why I have been suggesting that the thoughts about God that many people hold is exactly where the challenge is.

Now there is some good news here. We're beginning to move in a new direction in our evolutionary process. Some countries on Earth have actually eliminated capital punishment—a device whose continued use had been justified by an old definition eye-for-an-eye idea of God—having decided that one of the most advanced minds among us (Albert Einstein) was on to something when he made the observation that a problem cannot be solved using the same mindset that created it.

We have taken other steps as well, that can move us toward becoming a more advanced civilization, and creating a better world.

Some societies have actually decided that females should have the same rights and privileges as males. Some societies have actually declared that people who love each other should be able to marry each other, whatever their sexual reality. Some societies have actually chosen to ignore the color of a person's skin in the application of its laws.

So we're getting there. We haven't "arrived" yet, but we're getting there. And our next step is to embrace The God Solution. We can do this by deciding anew and agreeing collectively about Who and What God Is. Then we can approach our challenging and difficult human relationships from an entirely different perspective, using an entirely different model, and make some of the problems we have created go away.

Maybe all of them.

Self-made problems should not be the bane of an Advanced Civilization. Advanced Civilizations move beyond that. The solution being proposed here—a New Definition Approach—is about more than redefining God as Pure Love. It's about a whole new way of living that *arises out of this new definition.*

To put all that is here into one sentence, we need to challenge humanity's most important idea if we want to change humanity's most important experience: the experience of ourselves.

I think we are up for it. And I think that's what's next for us.

Summing Up—
and Looking Ahead

by Ervin Laszlo

T he chapters in this book convey various approaches to a better world—to an epoch we call "an era of well-being." By well-being we mean a condition of being well not just for the individual, but for all people and all things around the individual. In the final count, as Chinese wisdom maintains, the well-being of one presupposes the well-being of all. To be truly well means that all are well.

Now it is time for me to sum up the conclusions flowing from these explorations. To do so, I point to the core of the diverse yet remarkably consistent approaches to an era of well-being we have marshalled. The heart and common core of these approaches is what I call "the royal road."

Can we find the royal road? Clearly, to take this road calls for major changes in the way we think and act. To head toward an era of universal well-being we need to change today's dominant mindset—we need a new paradigm for our thinking and acting. Currently the bulk of the human family is far from concerned with the well-being of the other members of this family. The dominant aspiration is to satisfy one's immediate wants and needs, without much concern for the well-being, or even just the bare being, of anybody else. That is to travel the old road, and the time for that is now past. Here I summarize some hallmarks of the new road—the royal road.

Wholeness, Love, and an Expanded Identity—To aspire to a condition of well-being means aspiring to well-being for all, and this aspiration appears to be a pipe dream. On a closer look, however, we find that it is embraced by many people, especially young people. It is supported by an old but now revived insight: we are not separate cogs in an enormous soulless machine: we are connected parts in a whole-system—the system of life on this planet. We are part of all that is, and what there is proves to be a quasi-living organism—a coherent, seamless whole. Today this is not speculation: it is cutting-edge science. Separation, Einstein said, is an illusion.

Yet humanity has lived with the illusion of separateness for centuries. Our fathers and forefathers created the world of the 21st century in this light. Not surprisingly, the world they created proved to be unsustainable. It is a world where I am other than you, and I come first. What I want is power and wealth for "me" and "mine" and I am not concerned with "you and yours." You and I are separate beings, and while our interests may intersect on occasion, it does not intersect necessarily. In practice, it seldom does.

It is well and good that the realization that we are connected is revived at the cutting edge of the sciences. Unfortunately, in the form in which it penetrates thinking for most people is inadequate. It is not enough to affirm that A is connected with B, if A and B have separate concerns and aspirations, and only use their connection to further their respective interests. Connection between us needs to be recognized, but it must not be unilaterally focused on what I want for me and mine. In this interacting and interdependent world what I am—what is me and mine—is thoroughly and fundamentally linked with what is you and yours.

To reach an era of wellness calls for more than external connections between you and me. It calls for connections that are intrinsic and fundamental; the kind that transcend the bounds of who we thought we are. When A and B are intrinsically connected, they are one and not two. This is important, because it has a critical entailment: if I am one with you, I wish you well the same way that I wish well for myself. When I aspire to well-being for myself, I aspire to well-being also for you. And when I love myself, I love you—because loving you is to love the system of which you and I are integral parts.

Evidently, what we mean by you and me is not limited to an individual. From the viewpoint of A, B is the whole human family. There are no "strangers" in this family—we are all members of the same family. We rightfully see ourselves as one. And think and act as one.

Expanding my identity to encompass you, meaning all members of the human family, is a large order, but it is still not enough—it is not yet the royal road to an era of well-being. Even when we identify ourselves with all people in the human family, we can still see ourself as separate from the nonhuman members of the community of life. If we consider ourself separate from any form of life, the ills and problems of the modern world rise up again—the alienation of humanity from nature, and the irresponsible exploitation of nature in humanity's environment.

Being one with our fellow members of the human family is one step toward an era of well-being, a good step, but it is not enough. Other steps must follow. That step is to be one with "Life"—written with a capital "L." With a capital "L," Life is the ensemble of all living beings on the planet.

We can experience being one with Life: This experience has been described by many mystics and spiritual people. The contemporary mystic Rasha, who transcribed her own experience of encompassing oneness in a book titled "Oneness," described this experience with the following words.

> The reality toward which you flow—effortlessly, if you allow it—is unbound by the linear concept of time and space. It is reality where physical perception, by the definition, is superfluous. It is the result of a melding, a bonding, a joyful unity of the totality of your essence in harmony with what is now perceived to be "others." Ultimately, there will be no distinction between the perception of "self" and "others." For all will be Oneness. We are that Oneness. We are the unity of All That Is.[61]

Taking the royal road to an era of well-being means that we feel our oneness with other beings: with all complex and coherent systems on the planet. Ultimately, in its most intense form this feeling gives rise to the highest form of love: to unconditional universal love.

Oneness with people and oneness with nature are not conflicting experiences. Life—the ensemble of all forms of life on the planet—is the embracing system within which we live, and within which we rightfully and correctly love.

When Albert Schweitzer issued his famous call for "reverence for life," he had in mind the recognition of our oneness with all living things: with Life. When we feel reverence for Life, we feel reverence for beings who are not external to us, not others than we are, but beings who *are* us. The Persian mystic Rumi said, we are not a drop in the ocean; we are the ocean in a drop. We are not only *in* the living world—the living world is *in* us.

Such insights and assertions have been dubbed idealistic metaphysics in the past, but they are beginning to be recognized as empirical science today; it is the new physics. The world, physical cosmology tells us, is a whole system; in an apt metaphor, it is a hologram. In this holographic world, all the things that "are," are in every part. The entire universe is in every atom. And so the entire universe is in you and in me.

Feeling our oneness with Life is not mere imagination. It is our feeling of real and intrinsic "connection with the source": with the one-system world that frames our existence.

Evolution—Mainstream scientists have been maintaining that life on Earth is a product of a stupendous incredible serendipity, a cosmic accident.* Random interactions for some 13.8 billion years produced the universe we inhabit, and produced us in the universe. Now we know better. Life is not an accident. It is a universal evolutionary drive that comes to expression whenever and wherever it has a chance of being expressed. Organic molecules, the seeds of biological life, have been found to exist even in the vicinity of active stars, where scientists thought nothing so complex as an organic structure could form and persist. On our planet, life appeared about 3.8 billion years ago, and it continues to appear and to evolve wherever physical conditions permit.

The evolution of life is an expression of a fundamental evolutionary drive in the universe, and its manifestations express that drive. Life is not merely a search for fitness. If it were so, our planet would be populated mainly by blue-green algae, amoebae, and other unicellular, colonial, and simple multicellular organisms. Most of these species have achieved a nearly perfect fitness, a rock-solid adaptation to their environment. In Darwinian terms, they are amazingly "fit." Nothing short of volcanic eruptions, sudden climatic change, and natural catastrophe could lead to their extinction.

Yet the biosphere is not primarily populated by super-fit organisms; many species evolve beyond the range of their optimum fitness to the environment. There are species that explore all the niches that could support them, even those that offer the

---

* The substance of this and the following section is discussed in more detail in Ervin Laszlo, *My Journey*, SelectBooks, 2021.

barest minimum of the resources required for biological life. Some so-called extremophiles tolerate extremely high (and others extremely low) temperatures, pressures, radiations, and levels of acidity. They have invaded and colonized such unlikely niches as active volcanos, deserts, and the deep sea. They persist in conditions that were thought to be lethal for living organisms.

The evidence speaks clearly: The evolution of life is not toward stability and fitness. Evolution on Earth, and conceivably in myriad other places in the universe, drives toward the creation of complex and coherent systems: integral wholes, organic ensembles of their elements. This is important to realize, because to be aligned with this evolution is to be aligned with a universal drive toward wholeness and coherence.

Alignment with evolution leaves its mark on living systems, and the more complex they are, the clearer the mark. When complex systems are aligned, they are well; they flourish. For the complex system of the human organism, alignment translates into health and well-being. This is ultimately expressed as a feeling of oneness with, and ultimately love for, all living things on the planet.

There are many ways we can feel our oneness—the foregoing chapters offered a fair sample. One way to achieve oneness with the world is to take the science-based approach. Surveying the findings of the leading-edge sciences leads us to discover that we are not separate beings. We are parts of larger wholes, ultimately, of Life in the biosphere. Another approach is to seek the wisdom of the spiritual traditions. The *Dao*, for instance, guides us to the inner path leading to the recognition of the "unity of Heaven and Humanity"—*tianrenheyi* (天人合一)— so humanity can be connected with the impetus of the universe.

There are many ways we can attain a feeling of oneness, even identity, with living things. We can follow the guidance of the natural sciences, or follow the insights of the spiritual traditions. Then there are creative approaches such as those put forward by the eminent contributors to this volume. Gregg Braden tells us that we have everything at our disposal to create a better world; we need only to make good use of what we have. Deepak Chopra suggests the inner preconditions of doing so, including staying centered, finding and giving support, valuing inner peace and quiet, raising our spiritual IQ, and cultivating our detachment, which is not an indication of our separation, but the truer apprehension of the world.

Scientists show the way with their observation- and experiment-based theories; and mystics and sages point the way with their spontaneous insights. The approaches are individually diverse, but they have a common feature: They all lead to the recognition of our intrinsic oneness with Life. Our connection, and ultimately oneness, with Life is more than a personal and meaningful feeling; it is now a precondition of human persistence on the planet.

Looking Ahead

The expansion of our identity is a realistic task. Many young people are already expanding their identity and evolving their consciousness, manifesting their emerging insights in music and prose, honing a new story and a new "feel" for the human family. Their example will spread, since it is aligned with the evolution of Life on the planet.

Unless a major catastrophe intervenes, we can foresee more and more people revering and feeling their oneness with all the expressions and manifestations of life, experiencing unconditional love for the world they feel is part of them—as they are part of it. This development will encompass ever wider groups and communities of sensitive and open individuals, becoming a force in politics, in the economy, in technological development, and in the care of our environment. Humanity's evolution will conduce to the highest level any living being can aspire to: to achieve well-being for one and all throughout this remarkably coherent, finely woven, but delicate and vulnerable web of life on this planet.

A Personal Note to Our Readers

by Frederick Tsao

MY MESSAGE

We are at a turning point, and we all have a choice to make. A new era is upon us, and in fact it has already arrived. You can see it if you look around for it, as long as you understand what the essence of it is. As this book has described in various ways, we are facing a shift in our worldview, a change in eras, and this new philosophical paradigm is that of oneness and holistic well-being. We need to work out how to get to the state of well-being as individuals, as whole societies, and as the meta-organism called Humanity. All the wisdom of Western science and wisdom of the spiritual traditions of China are available to us as we navigate this transition.

The task before us is to enter a new era in our Journey of Life. It is a journey of awakening, of naturally aligning with the energy of the universe and creating the new era. To go on the journey and to awaken means that our creativity is unleashed and flows through us because all is life and life is all. We can add value to the whole system called Life.

Evolution will always point towards the challenge of the era, and the dominant challenge of our era is sustainability. At the same time, a new paradigm is emerging, one of a new consciousness that bridges physics and metaphysics. And we have the rise of China creating a new system based on a culture related to the Quantum Paradigm at a time when we are going through global integration. We are moving from a very divisive reality toward a world of collaboration. Artificial intelligence and other technological advances are expressions of the evolutionary shift taking place, and they support the dawn of this new era toward well-being. Quantum Leadership is about tapping into our inner creativity. In this life journey we are about nothing less than consciously working our way toward awakening and aligning with our inner force to collaborate and create a new humanity—a humanity that evolves toward flourishing, meeting the sustainability challenge.

The consciousness generated by this awakening, the new energy of creativity comes from the quantum level of our basic nature, from our soul. And we need that creativity to face the future. Technology-advancement is also empowering the emergence of a new system, and artificial intelligence will certainly take over most of the productive work that humans are doing now, and it will do it more efficiently and more accurately. In a world where AI has redefined the marketplace, all engagement will involve creativity in one form or another. Creativity will be the main thing human beings will need to offer.

We, the authors, as well as our contributors, agree on the direction to go: The Journey of Life is toward humanity's well-being. We are unanimous that the trends are set, and the time for change is now. The human race has reached a crossroads. We have achieved affluence as a species, but our life as a system is in grave danger. We now recognize the challenge to our future, and we have the choice to go on the journey of awakening, shifting our consciousness and alignment to create a new humanity that includes a new economics and therefore new politics and new social structure. The choices we make at this juncture, collectively and individually, impact on everything, but most practically on economics—the activity that responds to human desires. The nature of economics will shift as we move from today's market economy by way of the quantum paradigm that will impact in turn on what we desire, based on a new reality and a new worldview. This is the journey, the journey towards natural alignment with the universe. And as we take the journey, a collaboration begins that will regenerate humanity.

Both the emerging quantum paradigm and the traditions of Chinese culture view the universe as based not on matter but on pure energy. Through consciousness, human beings play a role in the evolution of the universe as it recalibrates and changes from one moment to the next. The quantum paradigm and the spiritual Chinese traditions both agree on the purpose of life and on the need for sustainability to provide a philosophical grounding for the new era upon us. The Chinese traditions also offer a clear methodology and a practical target. When everything that is natural and is as it is supposed to be, there is no stress; there is just being. Then everything is well.

The signs are clear that the level of consciousness of people around the world, particularly of the younger generation, is rising. There is an awareness, highlighted and reinforced by the COVID-19 pandemic, that we are facing problems that threaten the very existence of the human species. We need to respond actively, using the immense creativity which comes from our own soul, to create a new era, almost a whole new civilization.

The world today is not well, and a new normal must emerge. Leaders will naturally arise to face our problems. There will be people who will observe and understand the trends and will rise up to advance the processes of awakening and alignment, of collaboration and the creating of the quantum paradigm. What emerges will be a total redesign of the social fabric, a metamorphosis of the human system. This will be under the stewardship of what we call here quantum leadership.

We need leadership from individuals who understand the dilemma and embrace its solution rooted in well-being, sustainability, and consciousness. There is a task for each of us. Do not worry about changing the world; just change yourself and the world will change around you. Focus on yourself and choose your calling, and your calling will find your role in a changing world. It will be revealed to you through your passion and emerge into your consciousness. There is something you need to do for your life that has meaning for you, for which you have a passion—something that gives joy and will also change the world. I believe this will be your cotribution to the era of awakening and well-being.

So do you, dear readers, see it? Do you recognize the signs of the new era and the need for basic change? And if you do, will you respond? These are the questions. The future is not determined, the recalibration of the universe takes place from to moment. What role will you play? These are choices you must make to be part of the creation of the new era of well-being. To choose not to be a part of the creation of the new era leads to decay and destruction. And staying with the status quo is not an option. The best choice, the one we recommend, is to be a quantum leader. Play a role and do your best to assist in the transition to the new era.

The path is there for you to start your journey—to awaken, to shift your consciousness, to align, to collaborate, and to create a new future—an era of a new and sustainable social, political, and economic organization for humanity. The decision to take the first step along this road is for you to take.

A TRIBUTE

My friendship with Ervin is like a tale of two wanderers, one in the West with a scientific paradigm and another in the East with a traditional cultural paradigm. A chance meeting in the electronic world opened gates to a meeting of minds that was the beginning of a friendship. We connected at times of chaos where a unified worldview for humanity breaking across lines of divisiveness was much needed.

Some years ago I came across a short clip on Ervin Laszlo produced by Giordano Bruno University. His focus on using science to study the evolution of our mind and spirit and the existence of invisible forces that connect the natural world spoke to me. The topic of the new paradigm he introduced in his video was new to me at that time. Ervin's insights provided a link to many of the things I was pondering, but did not quite understand. I had an epiphany, where the dots of the various worldviews and cultures that I was familiar with connected and lit up. I saw a unifying opportunity in Ervin's work that can link humanity in a unified energy for all. And when I comprehended his insights, I could instantly see the value and the potential impact of the new paradigm on humanity. I knew immediately that I needed to meet Ervin Laszlo.

This meeting took awhile, since he was always on the road and so was I. He travelled so much that I was not even sure where he lived. Finally, one day it just happened; the stars aligned when I took a trip to London and heard that he was also there. I called Ervin to ask if it was possible for us to meet.

It was in the middle of winter when I finally received an invitation from Ervin to meet in Montescudaio, a village of a thousand people near his home in Italy. It was there that we introduced ourselves, and a meeting planned for a few hours turned into an exchange of ideas on many topics that went on for two full days. Those days were the start of a friendship that would bring us together for many joint projects and collaborations.

Ervin is a very dedicated man, serious about his mission, and is fortunate to have a super-efficient organism, an operating system with the heart, mind, and energy of a person in his twenties.

He is committed to creating the new paradigm and promoting humankind's discovery of the new worldview. I believe this is crucial to uniting us in the new era. It is a worldview that crosses the dividing lines of physics and metaphysics, providing links to the mysteries of the spiritual realm and answers to existential questions that conventional science cannot answer.

Since our first meeting we have met many times in Asia and Europe, and participated in many retreats together. I've had the pleasure of contributing the Eastern perspective to many of Ervin's books. He introduced me to his elder son Chris Laszlo, with whom I co-authored the book *Quantum Leadership: New Consciousness in Business* published by Stanford University Press in 2019. I then had the honor of inviting Ervin to present his insights on "Shifting to a Harmonious World" in Suzhou, China, on the occasion of the event I hosted there, the 2018 *At One* International Conference, dedicated to the creation of a common destiny for humanity.

Allow me to conclude. I totally agreed with Ervin's message:

> "The status quo is not an option . . . and nothing less than a complete mindset change will do. There is no outside authority that could impose it—it must be universal, and it must come from the inside. . . . it comes from the instincts and intuitions that have always guided human survival at critical points . . . [and today they are] signaled by the mounting interest in two factors: healing and spirituality. Both are crucially dependent on the evolution of our consciousness. The positive development in this regard is the rapid rise of

interest in the evolution of consciousness, and the insertion of consciousness in the processes that decide our future."

Ervin's insight resonated deeply in me. Of course, much has developed since then, especially with the impact of COVID-19 on the global system. The time has come when the new paradigm and new consciousness that Ervin has been advocating becomes clearly relevant. With Ervin, I discovered the relationship and common ground of the evolutionary energy of life and creation, the unifying energy that Ervin describes as the source. It corresponds to the concept of *Dao* in Eastern culture. There is the outside journey led by science, and the parallel inside journey guided by our cultural traditions.

Ervin's work is the scientific key to a unifying worldview as the foundation to define a new economic paradigm for the 21st century. His work is also the key that opens the door to the development of a common language, capable of integrating humanity as one system. I salute his wisdom that prompts him to continue to dedicate his life to create the new quantum paradigm for the world, working with and through the Laszlo Institute.

To continue his and my efforts to bring our work to the world, we have embarked on a three-year collaboration to ground the quantum paradigm and its worldview in practical applications. We are dedicated to developing a scientific language based on the quantum view as the new language to interface culture, belief systems, faith, and lifestyle so as to make this new paradigm accessible to all humanity. Our collaboration will continue to dedicate efforts to research and publish works that can bring about the needed shift in consciousness, redefining a new economic, social, and cultural quantum paradigm in a new era of well-being. Our coauthored book has occurred at the same time as he is writing his intellectual/spiritual autobiography, *My Journey,* recounting the three "incarnations" that have marked his life.

I would like to dedicate our collaboration to a fourth incarnation in Ervin's life, an incarnation where he defines a unified scientific language for a new economic-social system to serve humanity in the era of well-being. My wish is for Ervin to enjoy a healthy life of 125 years and more, so we could continue for a long time to benefit from his wisdom.

Biographies of Authors and Contributors

photo © by Bernard F. Stehle

ERVIN LASZLO

Ervin Laszlo was born and raised in Budapest. He was a celebrated child prodigy whose public appearances as a pianist began at the age of nine. When he received a Grand Prize at the international music competition in Geneva, he was allowed to cross the Iron Curtain and begin an international concert career, first in Europe and then in America. At the initiative of Senator Claude Pepper of Florida, he was awarded United States citizenship before his 21st birthday by an Act of Congress, Laszlo received the Sorbonne's highest degree, the *Doctorat ès Lettres et Sciences*

Humaines in 1970. Shifting to the life of a scientist and humanist, he lectured and taught at universities in the United States, including Yale, Princeton, Northwestern, the University of Houston, and the State University of New York. Following his work on modeling the future evolution of world order at Princeton, he was asked to produce a report for the Club of Rome, of which he was a member. In the late 70s and early 80s, Laszlo ran global projects at the United Nations Institute for Training and Research at the request of the Secretary-General. In the 1990s his research led him to the discovery of the Akashic Field, which he has continued to study and expound on ever since.

The author, coauthor, or editor of more than 100 books that have appeared in 24 languages, Ervin Laszlo has also published several hundred papers and articles in scientific journals and popular magazines. His autobiography was published in June 2011 under the title *Simply Genius! And Other Tales from my Life.* Gaia TV produced a special series on his life in the Heritage cycle, and he was the subject of a one-hour PBS television special titled *Ervin Laszlo: Life of a Modern-Day Genius.* He is a member of numerous scientific bodies, including the International Academy of Science, the World Academy of Art and Science, the International Academy of Philosophy of Science, and the International Medici Academy. He was elected member of the Hungarian Academy of Science in 2010. He is Founder and President of The Club of Budapest, an international organization established in 1993 that stands for planetary consciousness and a mission to be a catalyst for the transformation to a sustainable world, and he is the Founder and Director of The Laszlo Institute of New Paradigm Research.

Laszlo is a recipient of various honors and awards, including Honorary PhDs from the United States, Canada, Finland, and Hungary, an Honorary Professorship at the Institute of Technology of Buenos Aires and Honorary Citizenship of the City of Buenos Aires. He was awarded the Goi Peace Prize of Japan in 2001, the Assisi Mandir of Peace Prize in 2006, the Polyhistor Prize of Hungary in 2015, and the Luxembourg Peace Prize in 2017. He was nominated for the Nobel Peace Prize in 2004 and again in 2005.

photo by OCTAVE Institute Branding

FREDERICK TSAO

Frederick Tsao is the fourth-generation leader of IMC Pan Asia Alliance Group, born in the East and educated in the West. He became chairman in 1995 and transformed the family business from a traditional shipping company to a diverse, multinational conglomerate.

With more than 40 years experience as an entrepreneur, Fred has worked successfully with business partners and governments in multiple markets across diverse cultures. Not afraid to push boundaries, as Chairman of Intercargo, Fred repositioned the dry bulk industry from a shipper to one that plays a role within the global supply chain.

He later founded Family Business Network Asia and is now the Permanent Honorary President. Fred served on the board of Family Business Network International, where he inspired the exploration of the role of family businesses within the global system.

Fred founded East West Cultural Development Centre in Singapore in 1995 to research on sustainability and modernity. His exploration into Eastern Wisdom led him to focus on Chinese esoteric traditions and Western quantum science. Both are paradigms of conscientiousness and evolution.

Fred has since published over 30 books in Chinese, concluding that we are amidst a major consciousness shift and at the dawn of a new era of well-being. He advocates that business should transform and reform our era. For this, he founded OCTAVE Institute, a comprehensive, integrated, life journey approach toward well-being.

In 2019, Fred coauthored *Quantum Leadership: New Consciousness in Business* with Chris Laszlo, published by Stanford University Press. Fred also contributed a piece titled "Reconnecting to the Source in the Mirror of Chinese Culture" to the book by Ervin Laszlo titled *Reconnecting to the Source* published by St. Martin's Press in 2020.

Gregg Braden

Gregg Braden is a five-time *New York Times* best-selling author, scientist, international educator, and pioneer in the emerging paradigm bridging science, social policy, and human potential.

From 1979 to 1991 Gregg Braden worked as a problem solver during times of crisis for Fortune 500 companies. He continues problem-solving today as his work reveals deep insights into the new human story, and how the discoveries inform the policies of everyday life and the emerging world.

His research has led to 15 film credits, 12 award-winning books now published in over 40 languages, and he was a 2020 nominee for the prestigious Templeton Award. He has presented his discoveries in over 32 countries on six continents and has been invited to speak to The United Nations, Fortune 500 companies, and the US military.

Gregg is a member of scientific and visionary organizations including the *American Association for the Advancement of Science* (AAAS), the *Laszlo Institute of New Paradigm Research*, *The Galileo Society*, the Institute of HeartMath's *Global Coherence Initiative*, *The Arlington Institute*, as well as an original signatory of the 2017 *Fuji Declaration*, the international call to recognize and nurture the full human potential and divine spark within each human spirit so as to collectively catalyze a timely shift in the course of human history.

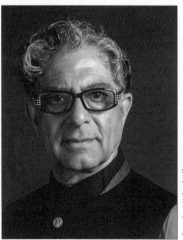

photo by Michael Allen

DEEPAK CHOPRA

Deepak Chopra™ MD, FACP, founder of The Chopra Foundation, a non-profit entity for research on well-being and humanitarianism, and Chopra Global, a whole health company at the intersection of science and spirituality, is a world-renowned pioneer in integrative medicine and personal transformation. Chopra is a Clinical Professor of Family Medicine and Public Health at the University of California, San Diego and serves as a senior scientist with Gallup Organization. He is the author of over 90 books translated into over forty-three languages, including numerous *New York Times* bestsellers. His 90th book and national bestseller, *Metahuman: Unleashing Your Infinite Potential* (Harmony Books), unlocks the secrets to moving beyond our present limitations to access a field of infinite possibilities. For the last thirty years, Chopra has been at the forefront of the meditation revolution and his latest book, *Total Meditation* (Harmony Books, September 22, 2020) will help to achieve new dimensions of stress-free living and joyful living. *TIME* magazine has described Dr. Chopra as "one of the top 100 heroes and icons of the century." www.deepakchopra.com

HAZEL HENDERSON

Hazel Henderson D.Sc.Hon., FRSA, founder of Ethical Markets Media, a Certified B Corporation. She is a world-renowned futurist, syndicated columnist, and author of award-winning *Ethical Markets: Growing the Green Economy* (2006); *Mapping the Global Transition to the Solar Age* (2014) now in 800 libraries. Her earlier books are worldwide in 20 languages. Ethical Markets TV series distributed globally at www.films.com. She created the EthicMark® Awards, the Green Transition Scoreboard®, EthicMarkGEMS®.com and co-created Ethical Biomimicry Finance®. Henderson served as a science policy advisor to the US Office of Technology Assessment, the National Science Foundation and

National Academy of Engineering, and she has many honorary degrees. Articles in *Harvard Business Review, The New York Times, LeMonde Diplomatique,* and journals in Japan, Venezuela, China, France, and Australia. An Honorary Member of the Club of Rome and a Fellow of The World Academy of Art & Science, she shared the 1996 Global Citizen Award with Nobelist A. Perez Esquivel. In 2007, she was elected a Fellow to Britain's Royal Society of Arts. In 2012, she received the Reuters Award for Outstanding Contribution to ESG & Investing; was inducted into the International Society of Sustainability Professionals Hall of Fame in 2013, and in 2014 was again honored as a "Top 100 Thought Leader in Trustworthy Business Behavior" by Trust Across America.

JEAN HOUSTON

Professor Dr. Jean Houston, PhD, is an innovative scholar, futurist, and researcher in human capacities, social change, and systemic transformation. She is one of the principal founders of the Human Potential Movement and one of the foremost visionary thinkers and doers of our time. She has been a key player in the empowerment of women around the world, and was awarded the Synergy Superstar Award 2020 by the Source of Synergy Foundation for her exemplary work inspiring us to source our highest human capacities. A powerful and dynamic speaker, and renowned for her gifts as a mythic storyteller, Dr Houston holds conferences, seminars, and mentoring programs with leaders and change agents worldwide.

She has worked intensively in over 40 cultures, lectured in over 100 countries, and worked with major organizations such as UNICEF, UNDP, and NASA, as well as helping global state leaders, leading educational institutions, business organizations, and millions of people to enhance and deepen their own uniqueness. She has authored nearly 34 published books and a great many unpublished books and manuscripts. Dr Houston is Chancellor of Meridian University and has served on the faculties of Columbia University, Hunter College, Marymount College, The New School for Social Research, and the University of California. Dr. Houston was also President of the American Association of Humanistic Psychology, and is presently the Chair of the United Palace of Spiritual Arts in New York City.

photo by Luigino De Grandis

BRUCE LIPTON

Bruce H. Lipton, PhD, cell biologist and lecturer, is an internationally recognized leader in bridging science and spirit. Bruce was on the faculty of the University of Wisconsin's School of Medicine and later performed groundbreaking stem cell research at Stanford University. He is the bestselling author of *The Biology of Belief*, *The Honeymoon Effect*, and coauthor with Steve Bhaerman of *Spontaneous Evolution*. Bruce received the 2009 prestigious Goi Peace Award (Japan) in honor of his scientific contribution to world harmony. For more information visit www.brucelipton.com

TOMOYO NONAKA

Tomoyo Nonaka is currently the Chair and Founder of GAIA Initiative in Tokyo, Japan. Formed in 2007 as a nonprofit organization, it advocates a shift in the core values of society and undertakes various forms of educational activities, community organizing activities, and support of programs for corporations.

Nonaka serves various other posts. She is a visiting scholar and lecturer at several Japanese universities including Chubu University, Shigakukan University and Shirayuri University. She has been an official member of the Club of Rome (Winterthur, Switzerland) since 2015 and served as an Executive Committee member from 2017 to 2020. She is a founder and a board member of "WorldShift Network Japan."

Before this she served as Chair and Chief Executive Officer of Sanyo Electric Co. Ltd., Osaka, Japan in addition to being a director or advisor for various large Japanese corporations such as Asahi Brewery, Mitsui Fudosan(real estate company), Nippon Broadcasting

System, Nihon Unisys and others. While she was serving as a Chair of a think-tank Nikko Financial Intelligence, she founded the foundation Association for the Promotion of Financial Literacy. In the 1980s and 90s she was a journalist and anchorperson of TV programs. At NHK, Japan's national television network, she had her own programs and covered many topics from international politics and economy to sports. At TV Tokyo, as an anchor she covered daily world financial business news in the show "World Business Satellite."

She has been a member of several government panels such as Council of Ministry of Finance that monitored the fiscal system with regard to the Japanese government's annual budget process and evaluated articulation for the annual budget, Central Education Council, Council of Ministry of Justice.

Nonaka earned a master's degree in journalism from the Sophia University in Japan.

photo by Christopher Brisco Photo

NEALE DONALD WALSCH

Neale Donald Walsch has written 39 books on contemporary spirituality and its practical application in everyday life, including the 9-book *Conversations with God* series. Seven books in the CWG series reached the *New York Times* best-seller list, the first publication remaining there for 137 weeks. His titles have been translated into over 35 languages.

Neale had been a newspaper managing editor, radio station program director, and nationally syndicated radio talk show host in the years before an abrupt turn in his life—a broken neck in an automobile accident and an interminable wait for an insurance settlement—brought him a year of living on the street as an out-of-work homeless person, an experience that caused him to explore the deepest questions about the purpose and function of existence.

He has presented spiritual renewal retreats and lecture programs around the world and online, focused on what he calls the most important question facing humanity today: Is it possible there is something we don't fully understand about God, about Life, and about ourselves, *the understanding of which would change everything?*

Neale lives in southern Oregon with his wife, the American poet Em Claire. His website is: www.NealeDonaldWalsch.com

Notes and References

1 Based on Ervin Laszlo, *How We Can Build a Better World: The Worldshift Manual* (Waterside Productions, 2020).

2 Zhang Dainian and Edmund Ryden, *Key Concepts in Chinese Philosophy* (Yale University Press, 2002, 72); The Culture & Civilization of China.

3 Matt Stefon (2016), Dao, *Encyclopædia Britannica* https://www.britannica.com/topic/dao.

4 Zhang Dainian and Edmund Ryden, *Key Concepts in Chinese Philosophy* (Yale University Press, 2002,179); (The Culture & Civilization of China) Explains the ontological necessity of *Taiji*. "Any philosophy that asserts two elements such as the yin-yang of Chinese philosophy will also look for a term to reconcile the two, to ensure that both belong to the same sphere of discourse. The term 'supreme ultimate' performs this role in the philosophy of the Book of Changes."

5 Chang, Q. Chin. Cult 4, 93–102 (2017) Translation of *Daodejing* in English: its place and time. Int. Commun. https://doi.org/10.1007/s40636-017-0083-4. *Daodejing*, one of the Chinese Classics, has the second-largest number of translated versions in the world, second only to the Bible.

6 James Legge (translator), *The Tao Te Ching, Lao Tse*, (The Floating Press, 2008, 78). *Daodejing*, Chapter 42: 道生一, 一生二, 二生三, 三生萬物. 萬物負陰而抱陽, 沖氣以為和。 https://www.daodejing.org/42.html as: "The Tao produced One; One produced Two; Two produced Three; Three produced All things. All things leave behind them the Obscurity (out of which they have come), and go forward to embrace the Brightness (into which they have emerged), while they are harmonised by the Breath of Vacancy."

7 James Legge, *The Tao Te Ching, Lao Tse* (The Floating Press, 2008). *Daodejing*, Chapter 25: 人法地，地法天，天法道，道法自然。 https://www.daodejing.org/25.html. Quoted as: "Man takes his law from the Earth; the Earth takes its law from Heaven; Heaven takes its law from the Tao. The law of the Tao is its being what it is."

8 Chen Guying and Bai Xi, *Criticism and Biography of Laozi* (Nanjing: Nanjing University Press, 2001). Describes "Freedom and Inaction" contains two levels of "Nature" and Inaction." "Nature" is a concept, attitude and value, as well as a state and effect; "Wuwei" is a kind of behavior, a means and method to realize "natural." The two are inseparable and interrelated. Therefore, to understand "inaction," you must first understand the content and relationship of the two before you can have a deep understanding."

9 Daodejing, Chapter 37: 道常無為而無不為。 https://www.daodejing.org/37.html as: Do nothing without doing nothing: "Doing nothing" means letting the flow go and not acting rashly. "Nothing but do" means that there is nothing that it cannot do.

10 Business Roundtable, (2019, August), Statement of Purpose of a Corporation https://opportunity.businessroundtable.org/wp-content/uploads/2019/08/BRT-Statement-on-the-Purpose-of-a-Corporation-with-Signatures.pdf.

11 J. Curran, "The Yellow Emperor's Classic of Internal Medicine." BMJ: *British Medical Journal*, 336, 777.

12 Huang Di Nei Jing, Su Wen, Chapter 25, *Discourse on Treasuring Life and Preserving Physical Appearance:* 天覆地载，万物悉备，莫贵于人。人以天地之气生，四时之法成。 http://www.guoxuemeng.com/guoxue/58951.html has: "Covered by heaven and carried by the earth, all the myriad beings have come to existence. none has a nobler position than man."

13 James Legge (Translator), *The Tao Te Ching, Lao Tse*, The Floating Press (2008), 47. Translated *Daodejing* Chapter 25: 故道大，天大，地大，人亦大 https://www.daodejing.org/25.html as: "Therefore the Tao is great; Heaven is great; Earth is great; and the (sage) king is also great. In the universe there are four things that are great, and the (sage) king is one of them."

14 Paul U. Unschuld, *Huang Di Nei Jing, Ling Shu* (University of California Press, 2016, 146, Chapter 8. To Consider the Spirit as the Foundation. The original text is as follows: 黄帝内经·灵枢·本神）天之在我者德也，地之在我者气也。德流气薄而生者也。故生之来谓之精，两精相搏谓之神，随神

往来者谓　之魂，并精而出入者谓之魄，所以任物者谓之心，心有所忆谓之意，意之所存谓之志，因志而存变谓之思，因　思而远慕谓之虑，因虑而处物谓之智。故智者之养生也，必顺四时而适寒暑，和喜怒而安居处，节阴阳而调刚　柔。如是，则僻邪不至，长生久视) In translation: "Heaven manifests within me as virtue; The earth manifests within me as q*i*; When the virtue flows and the q*i* has joined, life begins; The origin of life is called essence; When two essence clash that is called the spirit; That which comes and goes following the spirit, that is the *hun* soul; That which enters and leaves together with the essence, that is called *po* soul; That what is responsible for all affairs, that is called the heart; When the heart reflects on something, that is called intention; The location where the intentions are, that is called the mind; If the mind longs for changes, that is called pondering; If pondering results in far reaching plans, that is called consideration; If considerations guide one's handling of the affairs, that is called knowledge."

15 J Ou, Y. Hua, "Study on Translations of Five Xing Theory of TCM and Its Core Terminologies, Theory and Practice in Language Studies," 2020 academypublication.com
http://www.academypublication.com/ojs/index.php/tpls/article/view/tpls1002203207. In Huang di Nei jing, the relation among Five Xing, Five Organs and Five Flavours (sweet, sour, bitter, pungent and salty) is fully stated. Paul U. Unschuld, Huang Di Nei Jing, Su Wen (University of California Press, 2011), 95, Shu Wen, Chapter 5, "Comprehensive Discourse on Phenomena Corresponding to Yin and Yang."

16 In this essential regard the *Dao* is the Chinese traditional expression of the contemporary science-concept of the holotropic attractor, as we discussed in Part One above.

17 James Legge (Translator), *The Tao Te Ching, Lao Tse* (The Floating Press, 2008), 130, Chapter 71). 知不知，尚矣；不知知，病也。　圣人不病，以其病病。夫唯病病，是以不病
https://www.daodejing.org/71.html as: "To know and yet (think) we do not know is the highest (attainment); not to know (and yet think) we do know is a disease. It is simply by being pained at (the thought of) having this disease that we are preserved from it. The sage has not the disease. He knows the pain that would be inseparable from it, and therefore he does not have it."

18 Paul U. Unschuld, *Huang Di Nei Jing, Ling Shu* (University of California Press, 2016, 47, Chapter 1.) The Nine Needles and The Twelve Origin

(Openings) describes the twelve origin [openings] as the venues through which the 365 joints are supplied with qi and flavors.

19 Five elements and its positions North, South, East, West and Center, see http://www.chueh.org.tw/ 五行風水/五行與方位. htm.

20 The *DaoDejing* is permeated by the idea of the unity of Humanity and nature (天人合一), starting from the concept of the *Dao* as the origin of all, where to be in unity with nature, man must strengthen own cultivation in accordance with the requirements of the *Dao*.
Website: http://www.chinataoism.org/showtopic.php?id=768&cate_id=516

21 Albert H.Y. Chen, University of Hong Kong Faculty of Law Research Paper No. 2011/020 (2011, Nov), The Concept of "Datong" in Chinese Philosophy as an Expression of the Idea of the Common Good. The concept of 'datong' in Chinese philosophy was developed more than two millennia ago in the Confucian classics.

22 Daxue, *Encyclopædia Britannica* (February 15, 2016)
https://www.britannica.com/topic/Daxue, (Chinese: "Great Learning") Wade-Giles romanization Ta-hsüeh, brief Chinese text generally attributed to the ancient sage Confucius (551–479 BC) and his disciple Zengzi. For centuries the text existed only as a chapter of the *Liji* ("Collection of Rituals"), one of the *Wujing* ("Five Classics") *of Confucianism.* When Zhu Xi, a 12th-century philosopher, published the text separately as one of the *Sishu* ("Four Books"), it gained lasting renown.

The Collected Works of Confucius, Delphi Classics (2016, Version 1), 4905, "What *The Great Learning* teaches, is—to illustrate illustrious virtue; to love the people; and to rest in the highest excellence."

23 The Association of Confucianism in Malaysia, https://confucianism.org.my/ 經典/大學/2937/,　大學之道、在明明德、在親民、在止於至善。*Great Learning*, Chapter 1.

24 Wilhelm, R., Baynes, C. F., Jung, C. G., & Francis Bacon Library, *The I Ching: or, Book of Changes* (Princeton, N.J: Princeton University Press,1969).

25 Ibid.

26 *I Ching*, 易经, Book 1, Part 1, Chapter 2 坤,　The Receptive.

27 *I Ching*, 易经, Book 1, Part 1, Chapter 1 乾, The Creative.

28 Robert Eno, June 2016 (11-12), *The Great Learning and The Doctrine of the Mean*, translated 格物致知,　诚意正心,　修身齐家治国平天下　as "Only

after affairs have been aligned may one's understanding be fully extended. Only after one's understanding is fully extended may one's intentions be perfectly genuine. Only after one's intentions are perfectly genuine may one's mind be balanced. Only after one's mind is balanced may one's person be refined. Only after one's person is refined may one's household be aligned. Only after one's household is aligned may one's state be ordered. Only after one's state is ordered may the world be set at peace."

29 Rutger Bergman *Utopia for Realists: How We Can Build the Ideal World* (Little, Brown and Company/Hachette Book Group USA, 2017).

30 Frederick Tsao and Laszlo, Chris, *Quantum Leadership, New Consciousness in Business* (Stanford University Press, (2019).

31 Foundation work in 1952 by Clare Graves, introduced by Don Beck and Chris Cowan and eventually adapted amongst others by Ken Wilber in AQAL theory.

32 Spirals are alive, magical, powerful and multi-dimensional (Beck and Cowan 1996: 26). Spirals have often been used to represent evolution and consciousness given the number of examples grounded in nature, such as seashells, cobwebs and DNAs.

33 Don Edward Beck and Christopher C. Cowan, *Spiral Dynamics: Mastering Values, Leadership and Change* (Blackwell Publishing, 2002).

34 Opinion voiced by Sir Martin Rees, Royal Society Research Professor at Cambridge University, and quoted by Andrew Walker, "Sir Martin Rees: Prophet of Doom?" *BBC News* (April 25, 2003).
Website: http://news.bbc.co.uk/1/hi/in_depth/uk/2000/newsmakers/2976279.stm.

35 George Musser, "The Climax of Humanity," *Scientific American,* special edition "Crossroads for Planet Earth" (September 2005): pp. 44–47.

36 Ibid., p. 47.

37 Ibid.

38 "2013 World Hunger and Poverty Facts and Statistics," *Hunger Notes.* World Hunger Education Service Website: http://www.worldhunger.org/articles/Learn/world%20hunger%20facts%202002.htm.

39 While there are a number of technical research papers on thorium as an energy source, I'm sharing this particular one because it is non-technical and clearly identifies the advantages and disadvantages of this technology.

Victor Stenger, Ph.D., "LFTR: A Long Term Energy Solution?"
Website: https://www.huffpost.com/entry/lftr-a-longterm-energy-so_b_
1192584.

40 The UN Millennium Development Goals 2015 goal for poverty reduction
was achieved ahead of schedule. U.N.
Website: http://www.un.org/millenniumgoals///poverty.shtml.

41 Duane Elgin, "Why We Need to Believe in a Living Universe," *Huffington
Post* blog (May 15, 2011). Website: http://www.huffingtonpost.com/duane
elgin/living-universe_b_862220.html.

42 Ibid.

43 Ibid.

44 Ibid.

45 Ibid.

46 Albert Einstein, Letter to Robert S. Marcus, political director of the World
Jewish Congress, on the occasion of his son passing away from polio
(February 12, 1950).

47 Ray Bradbury, "G. B. S. Mark V," in *I Sing the Body Electric! And Other
Stories* (New York: HarperPerennial, 2001), p. 275.

48 World Wildlife Foundation Living Planet Report (2020) Website: https://
livingplanet.panda.org/en-us/

49 Nafeez Ahmed, NASA: "Industrial Civilization Headed for 'Irreversible
Collapse,' *The Guardian*, March 14, 2014.

50 News Insider, "The Earth can no longer sustain us," March 30, 2005.
Website: http://www.newsinsider.org/64/the-earth-can-no-longer-sustain-us/.

51 Tim Kastelle, "To Create the Future, We Must Understand the Past," from
The Discipline of Innovation.
Website: http://timkastelle.org/blog/2014/04/to-create-the-future-we-must
-understand-the-past/.

52 Steve Bruce, "Christianity in Britain, R.I.P." Society of Religion 62:191-203
(2001).

53 B. Starfield, "Is US Health Really the Best in the World?" *Journal of the
American Medical Association* 284(4): 483–485 (2000). *See also* M. A
Makary and M. Danie, "Medical Error—The Third Leading Cause of Death
in the US," *British Medical Journal* 353:i2139 (2016).

54 Richard Conn Henry, "The Mental Universe." *Nature* 436: 29, 2005.

55 Bruce H. Lipton, Chapter 5, *The Biology of Belief 10th Anniversary Edition* (Hay House: Carlsbad, CA, 2016).

56 Elizabeth Renter, "Blame Genetics?: 'Flawed Genes' Cause Less Than 1 percent of All Diseases," Natural Society (2013).
    Website: https://naturalsociety.com/still-blaming-your-genes-for-your-health -think-again/.

57 WebMD (2017) "The Effects of Stress on Your Body"
    Website: https://www.webmd.com/balance/stress-management/effects-of -stress-on-your-body.

58 Bruce H. Lipton, Chapter 5, *The Biology of Belief 10th Anniversary Edition* (Hay House: Carlsbad, CA., 2016).

59 Marianne Szegedy-Maszak, "Mysteries of the Mind: Your Unconscious Is Making Your Everyday Decisions," *U.S. News & World Report*, February 28, 2005.

60 Bruce H. Lipton, Chapter 4, *The Honeymoon Effect: The Science of Creating Heaven on Earth* (Hay House: Carlsbad, CA., 2013).

61 Rasha, *Oneness* (Earthstar Press: Santa Fe, NM, 2003).

Index